THIS BOOK BELONGS TO:

_____

I AM _____ YEARS OLD.

TODAY'S DATE:

_____

THE
GIRL'S
GUIDE TO
PUBERTY

THE GIRL'S GUIDE TO PUBERTY

Learn Personal Care as You Grow Up

SHANICIA BOSWELL

mango
PUBLISHING GROUP

CORAL GABLES

For permission requests, please contact the publisher at:
Mango Publishing Group
2850 S Douglas Road, 2nd Floor
Coral Gables, FL 33134 USA
info@mango.bz

For special orders, quantity sales, course adoptions and corporate sales, please email the publisher at sales@mango.bz. For trade and wholesale sales, please contact Ingram Publisher Services at customer.service@ingramcontent.com or +1.800.509.4887.

Girl's Guide to Puberty: Learn Personal Care as You Grow Up

ISBN: (print) 978-1-64250-967-0, (ebook) 978-1-64250-968-7
BISAC category code: YAN024080, YOUNG ADULT NONFICTION / Health & Daily Living / Sexuality & Pregnancy

Printed in the United States of America

Dedicated to Kamryn Amelia Banks,
my Sunshine who makes my world go round.

TABLE OF CONTENTS

FOREWORD

If I could go back and tell my younger self one thing about puberty, I'd tell her, "It gets better, and you'll be just fine." But time travel isn't real (yet), and I don't know if sharing that one bit of encouragement would be enough to change my puberty experience.

You see, I was devastated in health class when I learned that periods last up to seven days. I literally had to hide my distress and confusion as I publicly came to terms with the new information. Where I grew up, I'd always heard women speak about their "time of the month," but they never said how much time. And they certainly never said a full week! As a preteen, I felt wildly unprepared for periods and frustrated with nearly every adult in my life who had withheld valuable information on how to navigate the changes that were already occurring in my twelve-year-old body. Although I started my period the following summer, it was that day in health class when I realized things needed to be better.

Today, I work as a Pediatric Gynecologist, which is a doctor who helps young women and girls with issues related to periods and reproductive health. I don't just see patients in my office, I also use social media and public speaking to educate people on puberty and periods. I believe providing earlier and accurate period education is one of the best ways to make puberty years more of a time of celebration and understanding instead of devastation and fear.

That is why I'm so excited about this journal. My friend Shanicia, who has been working for years to normalize period conversations, has now authored a period journal specifically written to help you. She has included nearly everything that I wish I knew at your age. And she doesn't just tell you what's happening in your body. She also tells you why it's happening and what to possibly do about it. This book is like a knowledgeable friend who has the answers to your questions but won't judge you or make you feel embarrassed for asking. Because you can move through the journal at your own pace, you don't have to be afraid of being overwhelmed or shocked by the information. You can pause when you need to and even reread sections until you feel like you better understand them.

My favorite part about the journal is how it prioritizes your emotional changes just as much as the physical ones. Whether you're irritated, happy, angry, grateful, relaxed, tired, or excited, you're reminded to check-in on how you're feeling daily. And because we don't always feel our very best, she also includes affirmations that are encouraging and empowering.

I knew education and support around periods needed to be better when I was just twelve years old. Many years later, I'm thrilled to see a book that will help girls just like you have puberty and period experiences where you are informed, prepared, and celebrated. Now I'll tell you something a little different than I would've told my younger self. It has gotten better, and you'll be more than fine.

—Dr. Charis Chambers

INTRODUCTION

Hi! My name is Shanicia Boswell, and I am the mother of a young girl just like you! Her name is Kamryn. And like you, Kamryn has *lots* of questions about her changing body, puberty, and her period. I wanted to create a safe space just for you to learn about...*you.*

What does "**safe space**" mean? It means that you are allowed to be as **inquisitive** (curious) as you like while exploring your puberty journal and be honest about how this all feels for you. You can also work through this journal with a parent or trusted adult if you feel comfortable. Believe it or not, we adults have been through puberty too! We know a thing or two and would love to be there with you as you go through this monumental time.

Here are a few housekeeping notes before starting your journal:

♥ You may come across some larger-than-life words in this book. Why? As you grow, it is important that you expand your vocabulary! Don't worry if you do not know a word in your journal. If you flip to the back pages, you will find a glossary of all the **bold** words and their meanings.

♥ Throughout this journal, you will have several blank pages to write your thoughts. Don't be afraid to get creative, jot down notes, highlight, and bookmark pages that have an impact on you. Highlighting is fun!

♥ We have some amazing friends who are doctors. Doctors are a **safe space** for the tough questions. Our good friend Dr. Charis Chambers has written the foreword to your journal and reviewed the information we cover here. If you have additional questions that are not answered here in your journal, ask an adult you trust or your doctor.

Are you ready to get started?

AFFIRMATIONS ARE IMPORTANT (AND FUN!)

Why don't we jump into a few prompts before getting down to the nitty-gritty? What are **prompts**? Think of prompts as conversation starters. You'll see many of these throughout your journal. Let's start with these three **affirmations** (or statements) about yourself.

My name is _____, and I like to

be called _____.

Three things I love the most about myself are:

_____

_____

_____

_____

_____

A few questions I have about my body and growing up are:

_____

_____

_____

_____

_____

_____

_____

_____

_____

_____

_____

_____

A few more housekeeping notes as you navigate (or explore) your journal:

I want you to become comfortable with affirming self-love practices. You are special just as you are! Let's break down two words a little deeper. What do affirm and self-love mean?

- ♥ **Affirm:** to make a [positive] statement in support of a person, belief system, or idea.

- ♥ **Self-love:** to put yourself first in a state of happiness and appreciation for every part of you that makes you...You.

Examples of Self Love Affirmations

- ♥ I am learning to love all parts of myself.

- ♥ Being different is okay! My uniqueness is important in this world.

- ♥ I understand that my changing emotions are completely normal, and I can always talk about how I feel with a trusted adult, my doctor, or a parent.

Write your self-love affirmations below:

_____

_____

_____

_____

_____

_____

_____

_____

_____

_____

_____

_____

WHAT IS PUBERTY?

Puberty is a special time in your life when your body (inside and out!) and emotions change. Don't worry—you are not in this alone. Every single person experiences puberty. Your best friend? Yep! She will go through puberty. Your teacher? *Bing!* They have experienced puberty. Your parents and your grandparents also went through puberty when they were younger. Even boys have puberty! For most girls, puberty begins to take place between the ages of 8 and 14 years old.

Does Puberty hurt? Puberty should not hurt, even though you will notice some BIG changes in your appearance and in your feelings. What causes these changes to take place? *HORMONES.* **Hormones** are chemical substances in your body that travel from one place to the next, letting your organs and cells know what they need to do next. These hormones make you grow from a girl to a teenager to a young lady and, eventually, a woman. Can I give you a little grown-up advice here? Do not rush it. Enjoy every stage of your childhood. You have *plenty* of time to grow up!

WHAT ARE SOME CHANGES YOU SHOULD SEE WITH PUBERTY?

There are 5 stages of puberty for girls.

- ♥ Your breasts start to bud. **Budding** is what happens when your breasts begin to develop. Breast budding is one of the first signs of puberty.

- ♥ You are growing upward and out! You will experience a **growth spurt**, which means you may become taller in a short period of time. Are you able to look over the heads of the boys in your class? If so, you may have already begun to spurt! Girls tend to grow taller and faster than boys in their teenage years.

- ♥ Look below! You may have pubic hair starting to grow. **Pubic hair** is hair on top of your vulva. Some girls can begin to grow pubic hair as early as 6 years old! Your armpits may be a little hairy too!

- ♥ Your baby-soft skin is now bumpy. This is called **acne**. We will talk about ways you can prevent acne later in your journal.

- ♥ Your **menstruation** (or period) begins.

!Pop Quiz!

Have you been paying attention? Let's review what we have learned so far.

1. At what age do most girls begin puberty? _____
2. I am noticing my chest is growing. This means that I am growing:

    a. Two extra bellies!
    b. Breasts
    c. My identical twin sister

3. _____ are chemical substances that are responsible for puberty and the changes in my body.

What are some changes you are noticing in your body?

_____

_____

_____

_____

_____

_____

_____

LOOK OUT BELOW!
ALL ABOUT GROWTH SPURTS

Did you know that most girls stop growing at just 14 years old?
How tall are you? Grab some measuring tape to find out!

I am _____ feet and _____ inches tall.

A good way to find out how tall you may be is to ask a few
members of your family. Pick three and ask them how tall
they are too!

My _____ is _____ ft and _____ inches tall.

My _____ is _____ ft and _____ inches tall.

My _____ is _____ ft and _____ inches tall.

The average girl is around 5 feet, 3 inches tall, but the beauty in
being unique is that we come in *all* shapes and sizes. Some girls
are taller, and some are shorter. This is okay! Remember what
we talked about earlier? You are perfect just the way you are.
You may notice that you are a bit taller than the boys in your
class. That's because girls get a running start on puberty before
boys! Don't worry; they'll catch up to us someday!

THE BEST PART OF
BEING A PERSON
IS THAT WE ALL COME
IN DIFFERENT SHAPES
AND SIZES!

How do you feel about your height? Do you compare your height to your friends and classmates?

_____

_____

_____

_____

_____

_____

_____

_____

_____

_____

_____

_____

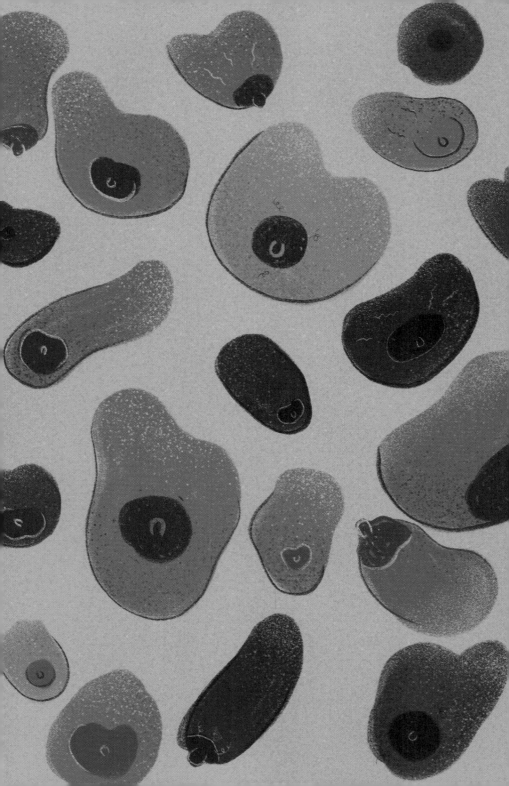

BREAST DEVELOPMENT

Breasts come in all different shapes—and when they are growing, they can grow in two different sizes! If the right side of your chest is bigger than the left, it's okay! They will eventually even out. Breast budding is one of the first stages of puberty.

STAGE 1: PRETEEN

Most girls start developing breasts between the ages of 9–13 years old. If you are at the beginning stage of breast development, your chest will be flat. You will notice your areola first and that smaller circle inside of your areola is your nipple. An **areola** is the dark-pigmented circular skin that surrounds your nipple. Areolas come in different colors and shapes too. If you are a lighter **complexion** (or skin color), your areolas may be pink or light brown. If you are more **melanated** (a darker complexion) your nipples and areolas may be a dark brown.

What is a **nipple**? The nipple is the pointy dark part of your areola that is raised. Your nipples will be flat before puberty. Once you start puberty and your breasts begin to grow, you may need a training bra to shield your nipples if they harden. Nipples can harden for many reasons, even because of cold air! What are **training bras**? Training bras are for young girls who are just starting to develop breasts. They are made to train you to become comfortable wearing a bra, not to train your breasts to grow. We will talk about training bras later in your journal.

The Girl's Guide to Puberty

STAGE 2: BREAST DEVELOPMENT

If you start to notice a bit of soreness around your breast area, it could mean that your breasts are starting to bud. As you enter Stage 2 of breast development, you may notice the skin under your breast becomes raised into a bump. This is the beginning of your breasts visibly growing. Your areolas and nipples are getting larger and darker.

Why Are My Breasts Sore?

The simple answer is that your breast tissue is growing, which stretches the skin. **Breast tissue** is what makes your breasts... breasts. Imagine balling up bathroom tissue and putting it under your skin. Each square of tissue is composed of a type of tissue that makes up breasts. These three main types of tissues are:

- ♥ **Mammary glands:** These produce milk for pregnant women to breastfeed their children. (You have *years* before you have to think about this!)

- ♥ **Supportive tissue:** Think of this as the additional tissue that supports the other tissues.

- ♥ **Fatty tissue:** Fatty tissue mostly determines the size of your breast.

Another reason your breasts are sore during growth is because of your hormones that stimulate breast growth. This can cause your breast to feel heavier on some days than others, especially when you start your period. You guessed it—we will discuss your **period** (menstrual cycle) in your puberty journal as well. Even though sore breasts may seem like a scary thing, it's not at all. Your breasts should not be sore enough to stop your daily activities. If you are noticing any extreme pain in your breasts, talk to a trusted adult or doctor.

STAGE 3: BRAS, OOOH LALA!

During Stage 3 of breast development, your breasts and areolas are on a growing streak! This is a great time to purchase your first bra. What type of bras are there?

- ♥ **Training bras/Beginner bras:** These types of bras resemble an undershirt but are cut short to only cover your breast area. Beginner bras do not usually have any underwire (this helps to support the breasts) and are not cupped (separated).

♥ **Sports bra:** A sports bra is normally shaped like a training bra but fits tighter. This is to prevent your breasts from moving when doing different activities. A regular bra is not ideal for wearing during sports and gym because it will not keep your breasts in place while you are active.

♥ **Soft-cup bra:** A soft-cup bra is a bra that is cupped, meaning there are two separate pieces of fabric that keep each breast in place. These bras are great for girls who have noticeable breast budding. These bras do not have an underwire and may feel thicker than a t-shirt. This is to prevent your nipples from showing through your clothing.

♥ **Hard-cup bra:** Hard-cup bras are similar to soft-cup bras, except they come with underwires and the cups are harder. Hard-cup bras may be better for girls with larger breasts. These bras give a more defined and even look under clothing.

♥ **Minimizer bra:** Are you not as comfortable with your breasts and want them to appear smaller? A minimizer bra may be best for you. They are normally shaped like sports bras with a thicker back strap to hold your breasts closer to your chest.

What Size Bra Do I Need?

Just like breasts, bras come in all shapes and sizes. Training bras, beginner bras, and minimizer bras normally come in standard sizes like small, medium, or large but soft- and hard-cup bras have numbers and letters. The number on the bra is your chest size, and the letter is your cup size. These may look like this: 32A or 34B. The best way to measure your correct bra size is to use measuring tape. If you are comfortable, a trusted adult can take you to a store where bras are sold and the salesclerk can measure you. This is done over your clothing. All you do is lift your arms! This is the best way to get the most accurate reading for your bra size.

If you have the measuring tape that you used earlier in your journal to measure your height, you can try to measure your breast size in the mirror. Take your measuring tape and place it right under your breasts and run it all the way around your body until the two pieces connect. Make sure you hold it snug but not too tight! You do not want to measure too small and purchase an uncomfortable bra. A bra should fit you nicely, not dig into your skin. Once you have your number, add 5 inches and this is your chest size. To measure your cup size, use your tape measure and run it across the fullest part of your breasts (this is normally right over your areolas). With this number, you want to subtract your chest size number. Example: If you measured 27 inches around your chest +5 inches, you have the number 32. If your second measurement is 34, you will subtract 32 and have the number 2. Your cup size will come in these variations:

- ♥ AA: less than 1 inch
- ♥ A: 1 inch
- ♥ B: 2 inches
- ♥ C: 3 inches
- ♥ D: 4 inches

Bra sizes typically come in even numbers but have adjustable hooks for your comfort. If you measure 35 inches, it is best to round down to 34. If you have 1 inch after you subtract your chest size, your bra size would be a 34A. Who knew that choosing a bra would be so mathematical?

STAGES 4 & 5: BREAST DEVELOPMENT

Did you know most girls do not fully reach breast development until the age of 18? That means you have your entire teenage years to develop breasts. Try not to compare your breast development to your friends around you. You have time! During Stage 4 of breast development, it can feel like you went to sleep at night and woke up the next morning with breasts. Some girls skip this stage altogether and their breasts grow at a more gradual pace. No matter how your breasts grow, you are perfect just the way you are.

Let's have a gentle check-in before we move on to the other stages of puberty. Now that you have learned about breast development, how do you feel?

Let's try an exercise. Stand in front of your mirror and look at yourself. Do you notice any changes in your body? How does your reflection look to you? This is a great time to use a few "I feel" statements.

Here are some journal prompts:

When I look at myself in the mirror, I feel _____

_____ .

Some changes I see in my body are _____

_____ .

Growing up makes me feel _____

_____ .

When it comes to talking with my parents about
puberty, I feel _____

_____ .

Do you have extra thoughts? Use this portion to write freely:

_____

_____

_____

_____

_____

_____

_____

_____

_____

_____

Have you been paying attention? Let's review what we have learned so far.

1. Labeling your body parts. Write the correct name of each part of your breast.

_____

_____

_____

_____

2. What are the 5 types of bras made for your breasts?

   a. _____

   b. _____

   c. _____

   d. _____

   e. _____

3. Measuring your chest to determine your bra size. If your chest size is 27 inches + the additional 5 inches and the fullest part of your breasts measures 34 inches, what is your correct bra size?

   a. 34C

   b. 36B

   c. 32B

DAILY CHECK-IN & SELF-LOVE AFFIRMATIONS

BODY HAIR

Why do bees have sticky hair?
Because they use honeycombs!

Here is a surprise you may have noticed already: Hair does not just grow on top of your head. In fact, hair grows in a *lot* of places on your body. Places like your arms and your legs but even a few more places you may not have considered—like your underarms and your pubic area. We will discuss your **pubic area** (the V-shaped lower part of your belly right above your private part) soon. For now, let's focus on your overall hair growth.

Is it normal to have body hair? Absolutely! Body hair is something that you should not be ashamed of. It simply means that you are growing up and your body is making the necessary changes for you to mature. Guess what? Your parents have plenty of body hair! Did you know that your body hair protects you from different things like dust? Yep. That's right. The hair in your nose, ears, and especially your eyelashes are there to keep your body safe. Hair on your legs, arms, and other places is there to protect the skin. If you are really hairy, then your body hair can also keep you warm!

HAIR CHANGES & TEXTURES

You may notice that your hair texture changes depending on where it is located on your body. Your pubic hair may be thicker and kinkier than the hair on your head. Your arm hair may be softer than your leg hair. The hair under your arms can feel wispy and barely visible. Your hair is unique just like you are.

Remember earlier, we talked about how body hair is normal and nearly everyone grows hair? While this is true, you may notice some adults and even older siblings don't have any body hair. Why is this? When you become older, you have the option to either keep or remove your body hair. It is important to know you should never attempt to remove body hair on your own for the first time. Talk to a trusted adult about your options for hair removal or if you should remove it at all. You are perfectly okay if you decide to keep all your body hair.

Take a moment and look at your legs, arms, armpits, and pubic area. Do you have hair in these places? If so, is the hair different or the same as the other places on your body? Can you count the number of hairs under your arms?

Describe the hair on the different parts of your body.

TO SHAVE OR NOT TO SHAVE, THAT IS THE QUESTION

There are two main ways you can go about hair removal: shaving and waxing. Neither should be tried without talking to a trusted adult first. **Shaving** involves using a razor pressed up against the skin to cut the hair down to the skin. The hair will normally begin to grow back within a few hours and by the next day, you will notice prickly hair has sprouted again.

When shaving, you want to use a good and lathering shaving cream to protect and moisturize your skin. Razors are typically safe but shaving on dry skin can cause skin irritation and ingrown hairs or hair bumps. **Ingrown hairs** happen when the hair grows under the skin in the wrong direction, resulting in a dark or painful red bump on the skin. Avoid hair bumps by shaving in the direction that your hair grows. On your legs is the only time you want to shave against the hair growth. Remember, talk to a trusted adult before attempting to shave. You could cut yourself and become injured otherwise. It is also important to change your razors. Do not use a razor more than 5–10 times. You can then discard your razor and replace it with a clean one.

Knowing your hair texture is also important when it comes to shaving. Depending on your **race** (the color of your skin as it relates to skin and hair texture), you may be more prone to ingrown hairs. If you are White or Asian, your hair may be whispier and softer. If you are Black, Native American, American Indian, or Pacific Islander, your hair may be thicker and coarser. Thicker hair tends to become ingrown more often than thin hair when shaved incorrectly. Knowledge is power!

Learning about what makes you uniquely different matters all the way down to how you may shave in the future.

What About Waxing?

The other way to remove body hair is by waxing. **Waxing** is when you use wax (wax is created by honeybees!) or very hot sugar to remove hair from your body. The wax or sugar grasps the hair, and you pull the wax back quickly to pull the hair from the follicle all the way to the root of the hair. The **hair follicle** is the shaft opening in which the hair grows through the skin.

Some girls experience fuzzy eyebrows during puberty, and you may feel the overwhelming urge to have hair removed from your face to give your eyebrows more shape. This is typically done by waxing. Do not attempt to shave your eyebrows! You may end up looking like a one-brow bandit!

Funny story: When I was in 7th grade, I wanted to have my eyebrows waxed, but my mother told me, "No! You're too young. Wait until you get older." I did not listen and tried to shave my eyebrows without my mother knowing. I accidentally shaved my entire eyebrow off and spent my summer without eyebrows. Moral of the story: *listen to your parents!*

The Girl's Guide to Puberty

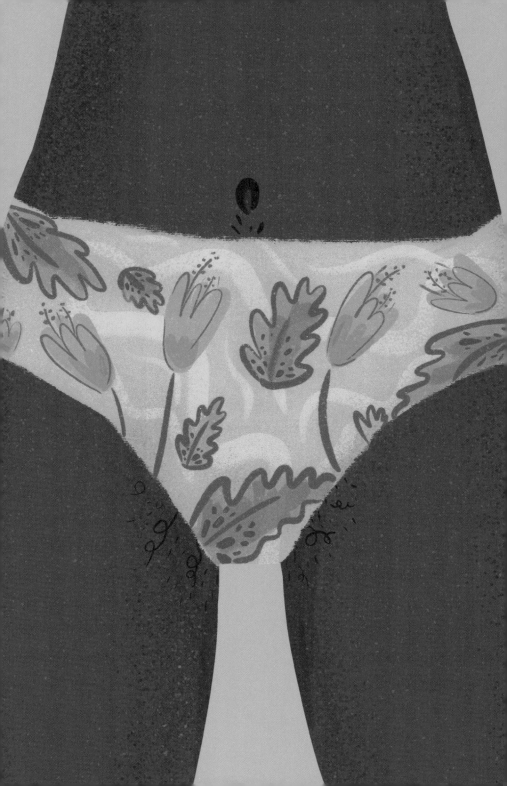

IS PUBIC HAIR "NORMAL"?

Did you know that pubic hair can begin growing as young as 6 years old? The average girl begins growing pubic hair between the ages of 8–13 years but if yours comes a little early, do not be alarmed. Pubic hair is completely natural.

What is the purpose of pubic hair? Pubic hair actually does a lot of really cool things, like protect your body from bacteria. Think of pubic hair like your eyelashes and nose hair. It protects your vagina skin from allowing dirt to touch your body the same way your eyelashes protect your eyes from dirt entering your eyeballs. Your pubic hair also produces natural body oils called **sebum**, which also protects against bacteria.

Earlier, we discussed how your hair texture can change on different parts of your body. If you are melanated, you may notice your pubic hair is much curlier on your vagina than on your head, arms, or legs. Your body is so smart! Your hair can be thicker and curlier below to prevent friction from your clothing and to catch the **pheromones** (or your body's natural odor through your sweat glands) that are released when you are active or hot. Later in your journal, we will discuss the importance of hygiene, especially during puberty and your period.

A gentle reminder: Your private area is exactly that: *private*. Using proper names for your sexual anatomy is extremely important. Let's finish up with the stages of puberty first, and together, we can learn the correct names for your private body parts.

WHERE MY BODY HAIR GROWS

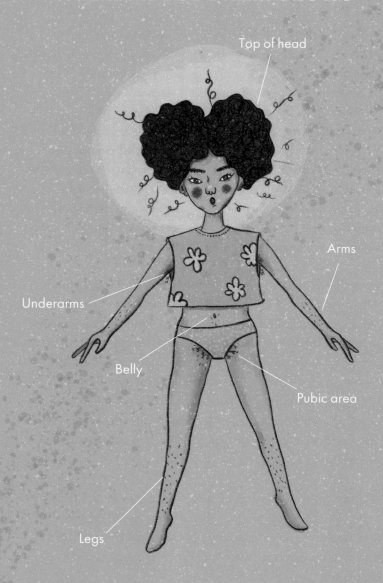

!Pop Quiz!

Have you been paying attention? Let's review what we have learned so far.

1. True or False: Growing body hair is completely normal! Everyone around me grows body hair on different parts of their body.

    a. True
    b. False

2. Who should I talk to about removing body hair from my body?

    a. A trusted adult
    b. My friends
    c. I can do it myself and do not need to talk to anyone

3. Keeping my body hair is a *great* idea! If I would like to remove my body hair and have gotten permission, what are the two safe ways I can safely remove my body hair? (Circle all that apply.)

    a. Shaving
    b. Waxing
    c. Using tape
    d. Letting my friends remove my body hair for me

4.   My body hair protects me from:

_____

_____

_____

_____

5.   Where are some of the places I may grow body hair?

_____

_____

_____

_____

The Girl's Guide to Puberty

DAILY CHECK-IN & SELF-LOVE AFFIRMATIONS

A CASE OF THE BUMPS

There is a special time in our lives that we experience what it means to have our inner beauty shine through. You may wake up one morning and not only not feel like yourself; you also may not look like yourself. What are we talking about?! A case of the bumps, a.k.a. P I M P L E S—otherwise known as acne. What is **acne**? Acne is what happens when your **pores** (teeny tiny oil-releasing openings on your face) clog up your hair follicles. Yep, you have hair follicles on your face. Oy, the joys of getting older!

Earlier, we talked about **sebum**, the natural oil produced by your skin. During puberty, your sebum production is at an *all-time high*, which can leave your skin feeling greasier than usual. Gone are the days of eating all the chocolate you want, rolling out of bed, and not washing your face.

A few things that can cause pimples are:

- ♥ Dirty sheets and pillowcases
- ♥ Consuming too many sugary foods and drinks
- ♥ Not washing your face
- ♥ Touching your skin with dirty hands
- ♥ Puberty!

Your skincare will become extremely important during puberty, and we will teach you how to take care of it during the hygiene portion of your journal. But for now, let's focus on those silly pimples.

Acne and Your Changing Body

The cool part about puberty is that you are getting older and will experience a lot of firsts in your life. Acne is one of those not-so-cool parts that nearly everyone learns to go through, deal with, and come out stronger. Your skin is just trying to figure itself out. Those fun hormones that cause puberty are also causing your oil glands to overproduce oil and sweat, resulting in dirt clogging up your pores. Acne does not go away overnight, so be patient. A good skincare routine, lots of water, and better eating habits will help clear up problematic skin. If the problem is too great to conquer alone, your family doc may prescribe acne medication to restore the health of your skin. Acne typically lasts from the ages of 10–19 years old but gets better as time goes on. Once you learn how to conquer your skin problems, the fewer issues you will have over time.

Here's something you may not know: Your favorite singer, YouTube creator, and actress have *all* experienced acne in their lives! Do not be tricked by beauty hacks. Even though makeup and camera filters can make our favorite celebs look like they're acne free, the reality is, we all have a pimple problem from time to time.

Acne can appear on many parts of your body but tends to show up in the places where you sweat the most. You may find acne bumps on your face, chest area, shoulders, and neck. There are a few usual suspects when it comes to identifying acne bumps on your body.

♥ **Pimples:** This is an umbrella term normally used for acne bumps on the body. Pimples can be sore to the touch and red on the skin. They are usually small and like to travel in **clusters** (or groups). Chances are, if you see one pimple, a few more will be joining them soon. Pimples may have a white pus-filled tip.

♥ **Whiteheads:** Whiteheads tend to happen when your skin cannot breathe. Just like you, your skin needs oxygen too! Dirt can get trapped in the skin, and without air, the bacteria can turn white, causing a small white bump. A medical term used for a primary sign of acne is called **comedones** (skin-colored bumps). Whiteheads are the result of closed comedones.

- ♥ **Blackheads:** Blackheads are the result of open comedones. Unlike whiteheads, your pores are open and filled with oil and bacteria, resulting in black dots or bumps on your skin. Instead of your skin lacking oxygen, blackheads are caused when the open oil-filled pores receive too much oxygen. This is a process called **oxidation**.

- ♥ **Ingrown hairs:** Even though ingrown hairs are not considered acne, it is important to include them in this conversation. Ingrown hairs happen when your hair grows under the skin, resulting in a bump. Ingrown hairs are typically caused by shaving and can be found on your legs, pubic area, underarms, or any other part of your body where you grow hair. Refer to our section earlier on shaving to learn how to prevent ingrown hairs if you have gotten permission to start removing hair from your body.

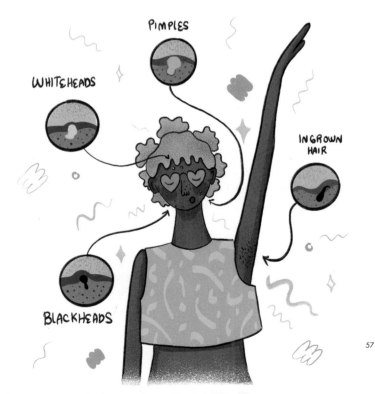

T-ZONES AND SKIN TYPES

Here's an exercise. Stand in the mirror and trace an imaginary capital "T" on your face, just like the image to the left. This area is called your T-zone. Simply put, your **T-zone** is the area of your face that includes your central facial features, including your forehead, nose, and chin. Your T-zone is also the part of your face that has the most **sebum** (oil)-producing glands and where you are most likely to have acne breakouts.

Our skin falls into 5 common categories:

♥ **Normal skin:** "Normal" skin simply means your skin is neither oily nor dry. All skin is completely normal—this just refers to your balance of oils.

♥ **Dry skin:** When your skin feels tight, especially after washing.

♥ **Oily skin:** When your skin feels oily to the touch. Your fingers may be shiny when you touch your face.

♥ **Combination skin:** Both oily and dry skin, this varies on your T-zone. Example: you may have a very dry T-zone but oily cheeks.

♥ **Sensitive skin:** Sensitive skin refers to skin that is easily irritated by products or stress. This skin type can be oily or dry, but most commonly, sensitive skin is dry, patchy, and appears red or swollen during an irritation.

During puberty, you may very well go through each one of these different types. This is because your skin is learning what is "normal" for you. Just because you are oily at the start of your teens does not mean you will be oily forever.

Determining My Skin Type

There are a few ways to determine your skin type.

- ♥ **Blotting method:** Take a piece of clean paper and press it against clean skin. Hold the paper up to the light. The parts of the paper that are translucent are where your skin produces the most oil.

- ♥ Wash your face but refrain from applying moisturizer. After about 30 minutes, look at your skin and see what areas are the shiniest. This is where your skin produces the most oil.

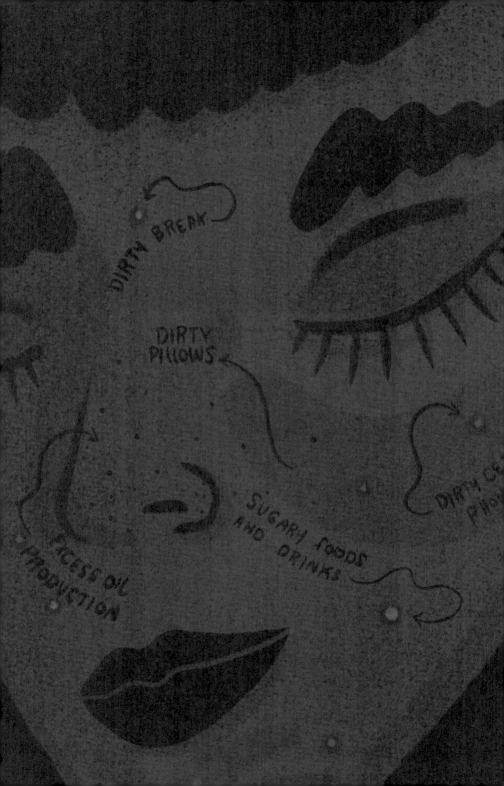

WHAT IS CAUSING MY BREAKOUTS?

A few tips on preventing breakouts in these areas are:

- Drink lots of water

- Wash your face well to remove dirt/makeup

- Wipe down your cell phone at the end of every day

- Change your pillowcases every few days. You can also get in the habit of sleeping on your back instead of with your face in your pillow.

- Eliminate foods that trigger a breakout. Say goodbye to those Snickers bars!

Later in your journal, we will go into more detail about how you can take care of your skin.

Don't Become a Pimple Popper!

As tempting as it may be, you want to avoid popping your pimples! Popping pimples can lead to skin infections and scarring, causing dark spots on the skin. When touching your face especially, always wash your hands first. Practice the 20-second rule: wet your hands with warm water, lather them with soap for 20 seconds, and then rinse. Instead of popping pimples, keep your skin clean by washing your face in the morning, before bed, and following up with a good face moisturizer. It's best to avoid letting your skin become too dry or else it will produce an excess of oil, which can cause more pimples. Pimples have a typical lifespan of 3–7 days. This can feel like an *eternity*, but it's best to let a pimple run its course and disappear forever instead of leaving a scar on your skin from popping them.

Rule of thumb: Avoid touching your pimples altogether. If your pimple problem becomes a serious problem, ask a trusted adult to make an appointment with a dermatologist. A **dermatologist** is a doctor who specializes in the treatment of your hair, skin, and nails.

!Pop Quiz!

Have you been paying attention? Let's review what you've learned so far.

1. What causes pimples? (Circle all that apply.)

    a. Clean sheets and pillows
    b. Touching your face with dirty hands
    c. Sugary foods and drinks
    d. Bathing
    e. Puberty

2. List the different types of acne that you can experience.

    a. _____

    b. _____

    c. _____

    d. _____
        (hint: one isn't considered acne but should
        still be considered)

3. What is the name of a doctor who specializes in hair, skin, and nails?

    a. Nutritionist
    b. Surgeon
    c. Dermatologist
    d. Veterinarian

4. How long should I wash my hands before touching my face?

a. 1 hour
b. 30 minutes
c. 60 seconds
d. 20 seconds

5. True or False: Instead of popping my pimples, I should avoid touching them and allow for them to go through a lifespan of 3–7 days.

a. True
b. False

6. What are the skin types you can have?

a. _____

b. _____

c. _____

d. _____

e. _____

DAILY CHECK-IN & SELF-LOVE AFFIRMATIONS

...PERIOD.

Nope. We are not talking about the little dot that you put at the end of a sentence. This "period" is all about menstruation. What is **menstruation**? In the simplest terms, menstruation is the shedding of your uterine lining of blood and tissue. I know this all sounds pretty *gross*, but let's break it down! It's your body, after all. The more you learn about what's happening, the less gross it will be...and the more prepared you will be for when it all happens. Every month, you will get your period. While it may seem overwhelming, it is important that you know your body's functions and the proper name for all your body parts. Like, what is a **uterus** and what on earth is the **uterine lining**? Let's look at the outer and inner parts of your genitalia.

OUTER PART OF THE GENITALIA

Genitalia: An overall term for your outer sexual and reproductive organs.

Labia Minora: The inner "lips" of the opening of your vagina.

Vulva: The outer skin of your genitalia.

Urethral opening: The small circular opening right below your clitoris from which urine leaves your body.

Labia Majora: The outer "lips" of the opening of your vagina.

Clitoris: The pear-shaped organ located right below the top of your vagina.

Vagina opening: The muscular canal leading from your external to your internal genitalia.

Anus/Rectum opening: The muscular canal from which waste leaves your body.

INNER PART OF THE GENITALIA

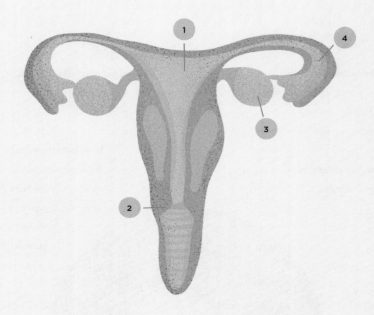

1. **Uterus:** A hollow, pear-shaped organ in your body. Also known as the **womb**. This organ is where babies grow!

2. **Cervix:** A canal right below your uterus that connects the uterus to the vagina.

3. **Ovaries:** The female reproductive organs that produce eggs. These eggs can produce babies.

4. **Fallopian tubes:** The pair of tubes in which the eggs travel to the uterus.

YOUR GENITALIA AND ITS FUNCTIONS

To fully understand your period, you have to acknowledge your genitalia and its functions. The reproductive system in a female is created to do exactly that: reproduce. Each part of your genitalia plays an important role in reproduction. Even though this system in your body is called the "reproductive system," you have many, many years until you have to even *think* about putting it to use in this way! When we speak about reproduction, you may be wondering what in the heck we are even talking about. **Reproduction**, when it comes to your body, refers to becoming pregnant. Your **menstruation**, or period, is your body's way of not becoming pregnant. This happens every single month, which is why your menstruation can be referred to as a **menstrual cycle**.

An important note: If you decide in your adulthood that you do not want to become pregnant, this is completely okay! We are just reviewing how your body functions and what your reproductive system does.

WHAT EXACTLY HAPPENS DURING MENSTRUATION?

Each month, your body produces an egg that can be **fertilized** (or grown) during sexual intercourse by a male partner's **sperm** (a male's reproductive cell) or other methods of fertilization. Even though you are many years away from having sexual intercourse, your body begins to prepare your eggs early in life, which is why most girls get their period between the ages of 9–15 years old.

Your body is extremely intelligent. When an egg is produced in your ovaries, released from your fallopian tubes, and travels to your uterus, your body says, "No pregnancy this month!" and the uterine lining is shed. This shedding of blood and tissue then travels down your cervix and out through your vaginal opening. Don't worry! The amount of blood flow is about 2–6 teaspoons and only lasts an average of 2–8 days. As your body becomes more familiar with your menstrual cycle, your period will last, on average, of 5–7 days. You will know when your period is coming to an end when your flow slows down, and the blood becomes lighter. Give it one additional day to ensure that your period is completely finished.

Let's take a deep breath and reset! This may all feel like a lot of information. If you are not already reviewing this portion of your journal with a trusted adult, it is okay to ask them to read about your menstruation with you if it feels more comfortable.

Does My Period Hurt?

Getting your period each month should not hurt, but it may be a tad uncomfortable. Here are some things you should know in preparation for your menstrual cycle:

♥ Your body will provide **indications** (or signs) that your period may be starting. Once you notice signs of puberty like breast development, growing pubic hair, and your changing emotions, this is a good sign to determine that your menstrual cycle is not far behind.

♥ Another indication that your period may be near is an increase in vaginal discharge. **Vaginal discharge** is a sticky white or clear fluid that comes out of your vaginal opening. Vaginal discharge typically begins a few months before your menstruation begins. This fluid should be odorless and colorless.

♥ Your menstrual cycle occurs on average every 21–35 days. A good way to keep up with your menstrual cycle is by keeping a calendar to mark your days of menstruation. You can count the days in between to be prepared for your next period! You can use a wall or desk calendar, or journal to keep track of your menstrual cycle. If you have a cell phone, you can also ask for permission to download a period tracking app. It is important to track your menstrual cycle so you can be prepared for the next month. Even though your period may not happen on the exact same day each month, tracking your period will give you a ballpark idea of when it may come.

♥ It is important to remember that when you first start your period, your menstrual cycle may not be consistent every single month. Your body is adjusting to this big change so your period may occur one month and not happen again for another month or so. This is normal. After having your period for two or three years, you will notice your menstruation occurs on a more consistent basis once a month.

The Girl's Guide to Puberty

Earlier in your journal we learned about your hormones. Your hormones can cause changes in your body, which may cause discomfort leading up to your menstrual cycle. We call these groups of changes that happen around the same time, or **symptoms**, PMS. "**PMS**" is short for "premenstrual syndrome." It sounds way more dramatic than it actually is, but when you are starting your period, it is important to know what to look out for. PMS can include these usual symptoms:

- ♥ **Menstrual cramping:** This type of cramping can happen in your belly and lower back. It may feel like a low rumbling in your belly that makes you feel gassy.

- ♥ **Diarrhea:** You may feel the urge to do the "doo" and go number 2 more around the time of your menstrual cycle. This is typically caused by your hormones and your menstrual cramping.

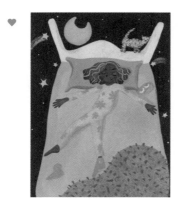

- ♥ **Fatigue:** Fatigue is a really fancy word for feeling tired. Your body is doing a *lot* of hard work, which may require you to get a few extra ZZZs at night and want to nap during the day.

- ♥ **Tender breasts:** Your breasts are a good indicator of the start of your menstrual cycle. You may experience breast soreness a few days before your menstrual cycle. You can thank your hormones again for this symptom!

- ♥ **Food cravings:** Do you have a sudden urge to eat chocolate? Your menstrual cycle can make you hungrier than usual. Be careful not to give in to all of your food cravings! You may desire comfort foods like chocolate, ice cream, and sugary drinks. But remember, these food items can cause acne.

- ♥ **Speaking of acne...:** Acne is another usual suspect and discomfort of your menstrual cycle. Keep your hands off and let your skin run its course. Hormonal acne usually appears in the same spot every time. If you notice a pimple on your cheek in the same place every month, this is probably because your menstrual cycle is about to start.

- ♥ **Mood swings:** We will talk about your emotions in a few more pages. Emotional ups and downs are a common discomfort in your menstrual cycle. If you are feeling especially emotional and don't want to talk about it, this would be a great time to start a personal diary or journal to express your emotions.

DEALING WITH PERIOD DISCOMFORT

Let's face it—no one wants to deal with PMS and discomfort during their menstrual cycle. Here are some things you can do for less grumpy menstruation:

- ♥ **Take warm baths.** During your menstrual cycle and on days of high discomfort, run a warm bath and soak for 20–30 minutes. The heat from the bath can calm your cramps and soothe your body.

- ♥ **Heating pads.** Just like warm baths, heating pads can reduce discomfort during your menstrual cycle. You can place the heating pads on your belly or lower back for the best relief. Talk to a trusted adult before applying heating pads to ensure proper use.

♥ **Drink lots of water!** Your body is releasing a lot of fluid and this fluid needs to be replaced. Drinking water can prevent dehydration during your menstrual cycle. You can also drink warm tea. Chamomile, ginger, and green tea are great choices when experiencing period discomfort.

♥ **A healthier diet.** Incorporating healthier food items into your diet can help with your period discomfort. Instead of grabbing a chocolate bar, opt for fruits, veggies, and nuts.

♥ **Walking and exercise.** Movement during your menstrual cycle can help with reducing the discomfort of cramping.

♥ **Rest.** Always listen to your body. If you are feeling fatigued during your menstruation, this may be a great time to take a cat nap in the middle of the afternoon.

♥ **Medication.** For some, period discomfort can be more than usual. If you are having an especially hard time dealing with PMS, talk to your parents, who may talk to your doctor.

Period Supplies

Just as bras are made for your developing breasts, there are products that are made especially for you when you get your period. These products are called **feminine hygiene products**. The five most common forms of feminine hygiene products are:

♥ **Pads:** A pad is a rectangular product made from absorbent material that is placed in the crotch of your underwear. The bottom of the pad is sticky, and the sides have **wings** (or flaps) that go around the bottom part of your panties to make sure the pad stays in place. There are many types of pads. Some are more absorbent than others, which means these pads can catch more blood flow. Some pads are longer than others, which is to support daily movement or to wear overnight so that your period blood does not stain your clothing or sheets.

♥ **Panty liners:** Panty liners are thinner and smaller pads that are not as absorbent. Panty liners are great to use even when you are not on your period to catch any vaginal discharge that may come from the vagina. If you have not yet started your period but are having discharge, panty liners can be used as a training product to prepare you for wearing pads.

♥ **Tampons:** Tampons are small cylinder feminine hygiene products that are inserted inside of the vagina to catch blood flow. Tampons normally come in a paper or plastic applicator that is inserted inside of the vaginal canal and pushed through the cylinder applicator, releasing the tampon. A long string is attached to the base of the tampon so that you can pull the tampon out to change or remove it. If you are involved in sports, tampons can be more comfortable to wear than pads because of movement.

Tampons do not create any bulging in your underwear like pads and are held in place in your vaginal canal.

♥ **Period underwear:** Period underwear is specially designed for your menstrual cycle. This underwear has an absorbent material built into the crotch of your panties or a pocket to insert a pad that allows your blood flow to be caught once it is released.

♥ **Menstrual cups or discs:** Menstrual cups or discs are inserted into the vaginal canal to catch your period blood. These are folded to allow easy insertion and then open inside of the vagina to prevent blood from leaking. Menstrual cups and discs are not ideal for your teen years and should be used once you are older. Please talk to a parent or trusted adult if you are considering using a menstrual cup or disc.

Pads, panty liners, menstrual cups and discs, and tampons come in many variations. It may be best to take a field trip to your local store to browse the different types of feminine hygiene products. A few variations are organic versus non-organic, which refers to the type of material your hygiene products are made of. The other variation is scented or unscented products. It is important to note that scented feminine hygiene products are made with deodorants, oils, and perfumes that may irritate the vulva. It is best to begin your journey with feminine products as unscented.

What Happens When "It" Happens?

1st day   2-4 days   5th day   5-7 days

Now that you have been armed with *all* of the knowledge of your menstrual cycle, you should know the signs to look out for, how to deal with discomfort, and which feminine hygiene product options you have to buy for your period. Knowing these important facts still does not tell us the exact day or hour of when you will begin your menstruation. The truth is, you may be in school, at a sleepover, or tucked comfortably in your bed the day or night your period decides to start.

The best thing to remember is to stay calm. Period flow can feel like a gush coming out of your vagina or it may feel like a slow trickle. Your period blood can come in an array of red colors, from a pinkish–light red to a vibrant red and even a dark brown. If you suspect you have gotten your period, use a tissue to wipe your vulva. If you are home, you may want to take a quick shower. After you have cleaned yourself up, find a trusted adult and let them know you have officially started your menstruation!

A great way to prepare for your period is to create a period kit. A **period kit** is a little goodie bag of items that have all of the necessary things that you need to face your first period with confidence. A few items you may want to include in your period kit are:

♥ A clean pair of underwear

♥ Sanitizing wipes that are safe to use on your genitalia

♥ At least 2 to 3 pads

♥ A congratulations card! You can have a family member pen a few sweet words to you that you can read for encouragement at the time of your menstrual cycle

♥ A bottle of water

♥ A pack of nuts or your favorite snack

You can create several period kits and place them where you spend a lot of time or in bags that you carry, like your school locker, backpack, family car, and your overnight bag for sleepovers. A period kit ensures that no matter where you are, you will always be prepared for your *big* day!

Your Period Is Not A Secret But It Should Be Private

The truth is that all girls have periods! You are not alone in these major body changes. You may have talked to friends who have started their menstruation before you or you may begin your period before your friends. The fact is, we all experience this life-changing event. Your menstruation should be celebrated, and you should not feel embarrassed or ashamed for starting your period. Some families have Period Parties for their young daughters who begin their menstrual cycle. A **Period Party** is an intimate celebration that celebrates *you*! You can make it into a pampering spa day, wear all red, and have cake and ice cream too! You can invite a few friends or just have your mother, sisters, aunts, and grandmothers join your celebration. Why? Because they have gone through *exactly* what you are experiencing.

Your menstruation is a pivotal time in your life, which means you are growing up. You are growing from a child to a tween to a teenager and eventually an adult. Even though this time can feel uncertain and even a tad bit scary, your puberty journal is here to familiarize you with your body. The better prepared you are, the easier this entire experience can be! This is why your period is not a secret. We all experience them and are thankful that we have them.

LEARNING HOW TO KEEP YOUR PERIOD PRIVATE

Even though your period is not a secret, your menstruation should be kept private. Your period products should be stored, changed, and discarded in a private place like a bathroom. Creating healthy habits around changing your feminine hygiene products and discarding them is very important.

CHANGE MY FEMININE HYGIENE PRODUCTS?

A good rule of thumb is every 3–4 hours. This means that you should always have at least 4 pads or tampons with you each day that you leave your home for school or activities. If you are wearing period underwear, pack two additional pairs with you as well. If you are wearing a pad, you will know it is time to change when the pad becomes full or covered in red blood. You may also notice an unpleasant odor coming from your pad or tampon, which means it is time to change. We will discuss good hygiene practices that are important later in your journal. Since tampons are inserted internally, you won't be able to check whether it is time to change them. If a tampon has been left in too long, it can cause discomfort. Leaving a tampon in for too long can also cause Toxic Shock Syndrome. **Toxic Shock Syndrome** is caused by a bacterial infection that can result in fever, vomiting, and a rash. Even though it is very rare, you should be aware. If you have a cell phone, set an alarm for every 3 hours as a reminder to change your tampon, pad, or period underwear.

DISPOSE OF MY FEMININE HYGIENE PRODUCTS?

Disposing of feminine hygiene products is very important. Never place tampons or pads in the toilet. Instead, wrap your used products in tissue and place them in a waste basket. Most public restrooms even have disposable tins for used period products. Your used period items contain your blood and must be discarded properly for the health and safety of you and everyone around you. If you are using period underwear, pack a few small plastic resealable bags to place your used underwear in to bring back home with you. Place the resealable bag in a non-transparent bag to keep your underwear private. Wash your hands before and after changing your feminine hygiene products.

!Pop Quiz!

Have you been paying attention? Let's review what you've learned so far.

Fill in the blanks! Write the correct names for your genitalia below. Refer to your diagrams if you need to!

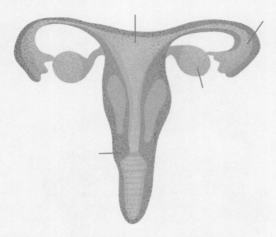

1. What is a period, as it refers to menstruation?

    a. The dot used at the end of a statement
    b. The shedding of your uterine lining of blood and tissue
    c. A mystical place in my dreams

2. What are a few indications that my period is about to start? (Circle all that apply.)

    a. I will have a lot of energy
    b. My breasts may become tender
    c. I will experience vaginal discharge
    d. I will catch a cold
    e. I may have cravings for chocolate and sugary drinks

3. What are some things I can do to combat
    period discomfort?

    _____

    _____

    _____

    _____

4. What are the 4 most common feminine hygiene products?

    a. _____

    b. _____

    c. _____

    d. _____

5. What items would I want to include in my own Period Kit?

    _____

    _____

    _____

    _____

6. How often should I change my feminine
    hygiene products?

    a. Once a day

    b. Once every 3–4 hours

    c. Once a week

Activity: Use this page to draw your dream Period Party. Include what you would wear and activities that you would like to do!

My dream Period Party would be:

The Girl's Guide to Puberty

DAILY CHECK-IN & SELF-LOVE AFFIRMATIONS

FACE & BODY CARE

What is the leading cause of dry skin?
Towels! Do you get it?

As you get older, you may realize that you have a new fascination with your body care. You may notice that your body odor no longer smells like sweet baby powder, but instead, your scent is offending not only you but those around you! Even though your personal hygiene can be a *big* deal, we don't have to make a big stink or fuss about it. Instead, let's learn how we can take care of our bodies the proper way. Let's start from the tippy top and work our way all the way down!

MAINTAINING A HEAD FULL OF (CLEAN) HAIR

As a young girl, your beautiful tresses can define who you are, and the cleanliness of your hair is uber important. Depending on your cultural background, your hair care maintenance can vary greatly from those around you. Here's something you may not know—your hair is special and unique to you! It's okay to recognize that your hair is different from your friends and classmates. We are learning to celebrate what makes us who we are and where we come from.

There are many different types of hair.

Your hair **texture** (or feel and appearance) can be straight, curly, kinky, or wavy. Hair can be black, blonde, brown, or red. Hair can also be natural, permed, braided, or weaved. Short, long, or medium, your hair is beautiful.

YOUR HAIR IS UNIQUE! JUST LIKE YOU!

You probably aren't as interested in wearing your hair in pigtails with pink ribbons anymore, and as you **mature** (get older), your hair care will become more of your personal responsibility. So, what are some ways that you can ensure the health of your tresses?

Draw a picture below of what your hair looks like:

FINE STRAIGHT
HAIR

Fine, Straight Hair

If you have fine and straight hair, your hair maintenance may include washing your hair several times a week, especially after sweaty activities and sports. Fine, straight hair can be oily or dry. As you go through puberty, you may notice that your hair changes between the two. If your hair is dry, you want to keep your hair clean to prevent a dry scalp, which can result in dandruff. **Dandruff** is dry, itchy, and flaky skin that can lie on top of your scalp. Dry hair can also be prone to **lice**, which are small parasitic insects that live on the scalp and live on blood. It sounds like a scary movie, doesn't it? Think of lice as very small scalp mosquitos without wings. If you happen to catch lice, which can be common in school, don't worry! There are plenty of shampoos that will get your hair squeaky clean and get rid of the lice in your hair.

Washing fine, straight hair can be done in the shower using shampoo and conditioner. A good rule of thumb is to lather your hair with shampoo for about 3 minutes, gently rubbing your scalp and your hair from root to tip, then rinsing. Follow up with conditioner. Most conditioners only need to be left on the hair for about 3 minutes. Rinse, then towel dry, air dry, or blow dry.

Fine, Curly Hair

If your hair is fine and curly, your wash day routine may be once a week versus every few days. Shop for a shampoo that works well for your hair type—preferably sulfate-free. Your hair can be "bigger" depending on your curls, and a smoothing shampoo and conditioner may be your best option for maintaining beautiful curls. Conditioner is a must for curly hair, as it tends to be dry. Leave-in conditioner is also a great addition. Right after washing your curly hair is the best time to apply curl creams and gels to hold your curls. You can either use the "crunch" method, which is using your hands to squeeze your curls in an upward motion gently to hold their place or use a wide-tooth comb to distribute product through your hair. Let your hair air dry or use low heat with a diffuser blow dryer. It is best to let curly hair air dry, though, as heat can be more damaging because the hair can already be more dry than oily.

Kinky and Natural Hair

Kinky and natural hair is typically washed on a weekly or biweekly basis. Your hair tends to produce lots of natural oils that are important for your hair texture, which can be drier than fine, curly, or straight hair. Specific shampoos, conditioners, and leave-in conditioners are necessary for your hair type. Young girls with kinky and natural hair may still have their hair washed by their mothers or in a salon to "train" their hair to grow healthy. Your hair is more prone to split ends and breaking so a good wash day routine is essential. "Hair Day" or "Wash Day" in the Black community refers to the day that we commit hours to wash and style our hair. This is truly a cultural experience. Grab a few snacks, turn on a good movie or grab a book, and enjoy the process! This is a rite of passage for many young Black girls. **Rite of passage** refers to an experience that defines an important event in life. Can you guess another important rite of passage all girls go through? Yep, your periods!

With kinky or natural hair, you can wear your hair in many different styles, from an afro to locs to a twist out, braids, or wear it straight. Your hair is as versatile and beautiful, just like you!

A FEW SELF-LOVE AFFIRMATIONS

I would describe my hair texture as _____

Three things I really love about my hair are:

1. _____

2. _____

3. _____

My favorite hairstyle to wear is:

_____

_____

_____

A hairstyle I would like to try is:

_____

_____

_____

Someone I look up to who has hair just like me is:

_____

A cartoon character that has hair just like me is:

_____

The Girl's Guide to Puberty

ALL ABOUT FACE!

We learned a *lot* about your face earlier in your journal. Now let's learn how to take care of it! Face washing is just as important as washing all the other parts of your body, but since your facial skin can be more sensitive and thinner than the rest of the skin you're in, washing your face is a bit different.

Washing & Hygiene

HOW OFTEN SHOULD I WASH MY FACE AND FOR HOW LONG?

You should wash your face twice a day! Wash your face in the morning with a warm, damp washcloth and before bed with a face cleanser. You may wonder why you need to wash your face in the morning after you have just cleaned your face the night before, but this is so that you can refresh your skin before leaving home. This is the time to wipe all the crusties from your eyes so they can shine! Washing your face at nighttime is very important. This removes all the dirt, sweat, and if you wear makeup, makeup too! To wash your face, wash your hands first then splash your face with warm water and make a gentle lather with your facial soap. If you are using liquid soap, one pump of face soap should do! Gently massage your face with your soap for about 20 seconds and rinse. Pat your face dry with a clean washcloth instead of rubbing your skin dry. Avoid over-washing your face so that you don't dry out your skin. Remember, keep your hands off your clean face after washing.

CAN I USE MY BODY SOAP AS FACE SOAP?

Typically, no. You want to use a soap especially made for your face instead. Body soaps can contain perfumes that are not great for the face and can cause breakouts. Depending on what kind of skin you have (do a review in the acne section of your journal), use a facial soap specific to your skin type. Face soaps come in many different forms, from liquid to **exfoliating** (a gentle scrub) and even as bar soap.

What's Next?

After washing your face, you can use a **toner** (a skin-balancing lotion or liquid), which can help reduce the size of your skin pores. **Pores** are tiny holes on your face that release oils but can catch bacteria and dirt. Toner can be sprayed on the face, applied with a cotton ball, or used as a lotion. Always allow a few minutes to pass to make sure your toner is dry before going to this next step.

A GOOD MOISTURIZER

Always follow your face wash and toner with a good moisturizer. This will ensure the health and elasticity of your skin. Make sure you use a lotion specifically for your face. Like scented soaps, perfumed lotions can be irritating to your face. Do not over-apply your face lotion! One small pump or finger-size amount should do. Apply your moisturizer in a circular upward motion and make sure it is fully absorbed into the skin.

Using sunscreen for your face can not only protect your face from the sun's **UV** (ultraviolet) rays, but it can also prevent dark spots and pimples. Look for a sunscreen specifically for your face versus a body sunscreen, as these can contain fragrances that can irritate the skin. Use sunscreen with an **SPF** (sun protection factor) of at least 30. This blocks out 97 percent of the sun's **UVB** (type b ultraviolet) rays.

What About Makeup?

Here's the thing: you are already beautiful! Do not feel pressured to wear makeup if you are not comfortable. Many women do not wear it at all. Remember, you should always have permission from your parents before using makeup. Let's go over a few of the basic makeup items you may want to try:

♥ **Primer:** Primer is a lotion that you apply to the skin that acts as a barrier between your skin and makeup.

♥ **Foundation:** Foundation is a liquid or powdered form of makeup that matches your skin to even out your skin tone and cover any breakouts or dark spots. An important note when applying foundation: less is more! Using too much foundation can make your skin look thick and cakey.

♥ **Eyeshadow:** Eyeshadow is a colorful powder that goes on top of your eyelids.

💜 **Eyeliner:** Eyeliner is applied on top of your eyelid behind your eyelashes to give your eyes a more defined look. Eyeliner can come in liquid or pencil form.

💜 **Mascara:** Mascara goes on top of your eyelashes to make them darker and easier to see.

💜 **Blush:** Blush is applied to your cheeks to give them a rosy look. Smile! You should always smile before applying blush. Use a makeup brush and gently swirl the powder to the fullest parts of your cheeks.

💜 **Lip gloss:** Lip gloss can be clear or have color. They add a bit of shine to your lips!

MAKEUP TIPS:

♥ You can apply your makeup with makeup brushes or clean fingertips. Make sure you wash and clean your makeup brushes thoroughly with soap and water every 2 weeks.

♥ If you experience heavy breakouts, it may be tempting to cover your skin with makeup, but makeup can cause your skin to break out more. Make sure that you wash your face thoroughly at the end of the night to remove all makeup from your skin.

♥ At your age, less is more. Always go for a more natural makeup look instead of overdoing it.

♥ If you need help learning how to apply your makeup, ask your mom, older sister, or another adult that you trust! You can also watch YouTube if you have permission.

!Pop Quiz!

Have you been paying attention? Let's review what we have learned so far.

1. Why is it important for me to wash my hair?

_____

_____

_____

2. What are **pores**?
   a. What I do when I want something to drink
   b. What happens when rain falls from the sky
   c. The tiny holes on your face that release oils but can catch bacteria and dirt

3. What types of products should I use on my face for the best skin care? (Circle all that apply.)
   a. Face wash
   b. Body lotion
   c. Toner
   d. Perfume
   e. Body sunscreen

4. What are the seven basic types of makeup? List them all.

a. _____

b. _____

c. _____

d. _____

e. _____

f. _____

g. _____

5. True or False: I should always ask for permission from my parents before wearing makeup.

a. True
b. False

DAILY CHECK-IN & SELF-LOVE AFFIRMATIONS

EYES, EARS AND TEETH

SEEING IS BELIEVING: EYE CARE

Did you know that you only get *one* pair of eyes? Your eye care is very important, so let's learn all we need to know about caring for your eyes. Every year you should have an eye exam to check the health of your eyes and your eyesight. An **eye exam** is done by an **optometrist** (eye doctor) and is a series of tests to check your vision. Your vision can vary from being 20/20, meaning you have perfect eyesight, or it can be determined that you need glasses or contacts. Your doc will also determine if you are **nearsighted**, meaning you see objects up close well but not far away, or if you are **farsighted**, meaning you can see objects well far away but not up close.

Here are a few signs to look out for that you may need glasses or contacts:

- ♥ Blurry vision
- ♥ Headaches
- ♥ Squinting to read or watch television

If you are experiencing these symptoms, you may need glasses or contacts.

Glasses Are Cool!

Glasses should be an expression of your unique personality! You can choose different colors and shapes to reflect who you are. Always care for your glasses by storing them in your protective case to avoid scratches to the lenses. You can also use a glasses lens cleaner to wipe away any smudges. Never use a tissue or your clothing to wipe off your glasses. These can scratch the lenses.

Contacts Are an Option

Contacts are small and flimsy round lenses that are inserted directly into your eyes to help you see. Contacts come in two main forms:

- ♥ **Extended wear:** You can wear these contacts for up to a month at a time before removing and discarding.

- ♥ **Disposable:** These contacts are inserted and removed at the end of every night, once every 2 weeks (or monthly) and replaced with a new pair of lenses.

Remember, always wash your hands before inserting and removing contact lenses. Once your lenses are removed, place them in your contacts case with fresh **solution** (contact lens cleaner) every night.

Did you know that your eyesight can be different in each eye? If you are wearing contacts with different prescriptions, make sure you place each contact lens in the correct Left or Right label on your contact lens case.

HOW TO PROTECT YOUR EYES:

- ♥ Give your eyes a break! Take breaks between your television and phone time.

- ♥ Never use a cell phone with the brightness turned up high in a dark room. This can cause your eyes to strain.

- ♥ Just like cellphones, take precaution when watching television in dark rooms often. It's okay to turn on a lamp when watching TV.

- ♥ Wear sunglasses when you are outside. This protects your eyes from the sun's harmful UV rays. If you wear prescription glasses, you can have your doc prescribe separate sunglasses or ask for transition glasses, which will turn your regular glasses into sunglasses when you are outdoors.

CAN YOU HEAR ME NOW?
ALL ABOUT EARS

Can you wiggle your ears? If not, that's okay! Your ears have a really important job as a part of your body. Your ears are responsible for hearing, which means taking care of them is a big job.

Your ears contain **earwax**. You may remember we talked about wax earlier in your journal. Earwax is similar. Only your ears make this wax, not honeybees. Sometimes, your earwax can build up and you will want to clean the wax out. Here are a few important tips on cleaning your ears:

💜 Never stick pointy or foreign objects in your ears. You can damage your **eardrums**, the vibrating membranes inside of your ears that respond to incoming sound waves. Consider your eardrums as your little **boomboxes** or radios.

💜 If you need to clean your ears, ask a trusted adult *first*. There are cotton swabs you can use made specifically for your ears. While cotton swabs are made to go inside your ears, you don't want to push them too fast, too hard, or too far. Once you've gotten the swab into your ear, spin in a circular motion to collect the earwax. An adult can help you use a cotton swab for the first time.

Earrings & Clip-Ons

Earrings can also be a form of self-expression if you have permission to wear them. Earrings can either be **clip-ons**, which snap around the earlobe, or **pierced**, which go directly through the earlobe. Your ears should only be pierced by a professional in a clean and sterile environment. Ears are pierced either by a small needle or with an earring machine gun. Ear piercing takes about 1 minute per ear and 2–3 months to heal. Make sure to clean your pierced ears as recommended by the professional that has pierced them and twist them daily as they heal.

Play That Funky Music!

We all love listening to music, right? *Right!* If you are wearing headphones, let's keep in mind our little inner boomboxes, our eardrums. Eardrums pick up **sound waves**, or moving and vibrating energy, which vibrate the eardrum. Hairlike cells convert these vibrations into nerve impulses and these nerve impulses are then carried up to the auditory nerve in your brain and *voila!* Your brain converts these impulses into sound. Who knew your eardrums could do so much work? Every time you hear a sound, thank your body and your brain. How can we say thank you? By wearing headphones responsibly.

TIPS ON WEARING HEADPHONES:

- ♥ Opt for full-coverage headphones instead of earphones that are inserted directly into your ears. This makes sure sounds are properly balanced.

- ♥ Do not play your headphones at the maximum level. This can damage your eardrums.

- ♥ If you are wearing direct-inserted headphones, clean them often to avoid ear infections.

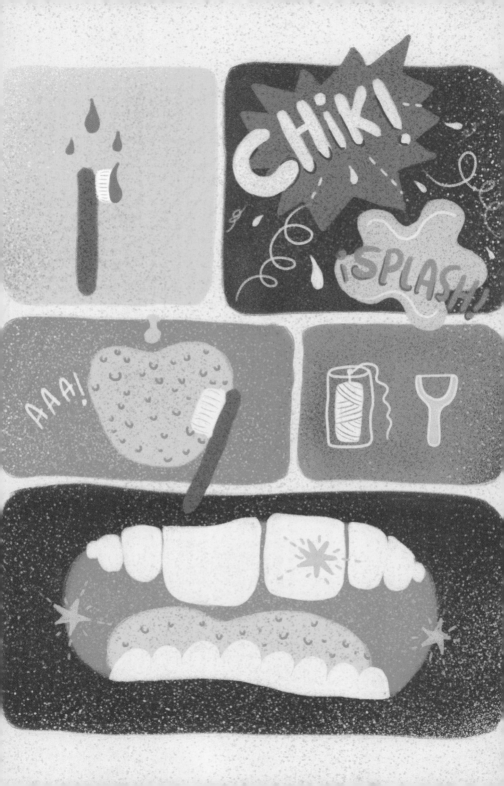

YOUR PEARLY WHITES: BRUSHING YOUR TEETH

Let's see those bright and beautiful smiles! As you become older, your **oral hygiene**, or the practice of keeping your mouth clean, will protect your teeth for years to come. Once you lose your baby teeth, your adult teeth will grow in as your final set of teeth. So, how do you brush your teeth?

- ♥ **Step 1:** Wet your toothbrush and apply toothpaste.

- ♥ **Step 2:** Brush the front of your teeth **vertically** or up and down. As you move to the sides and back of your mouth, brush **horizontally** or side to side.

- ♥ **Step 3:** Brush your gums gently.

- ♥ **Step 4:** Stick your tongue out and brush from the tip of your tongue all the way to the back. This is where the bad breath is! Brush under your tongue too.

- ♥ **Step 5:** Use floss to clean between your teeth.

- ♥ **Step 6:** Rinse your mouth with warm water or mouthwash. Rinse your toothbrush with warm water.

Why should you brush your teeth? Brushing your teeth is preventive care. Not brushing your teeth can lead to:

- ♥ **Cavities:** Rotten holes in your teeth caused by sugar, bacteria, candy, and soda/juices.

- ♥ **Plaque buildup:** A sticky film of bacteria that forms across the teeth. Once hardened, plaque can be difficult to remove.

- ♥ **Yellow teeth:** This happens when the **enamel,** or the thin outer covering of your teeth, becomes worn or not properly cleaned, causing a yellow tooth stain.

- ♥ **Bad breath:** This happens when your tongue isn't brushed properly or old food isn't removed through brushing. Extremely bad breath can be caused by **halitosis**, which is *really* bad breath not caused by poor dental habits. You may need to see a dentist if your breath is unpleasant, even with proper mouth cleaning. Bad breath can also come from **dehydration** or lack of water.

- ♥ **Gingivitis:** Gum disease, which causes swollen, red, and inflamed gums.

It's better to be safe than sorry here! Make sure you brush your teeth twice a day, at least 2 minutes each time.

If you have taken a trip to the dentist, then you are familiar with teeth hygiene. As your adult teeth begin to grow, your dentist may see early signs that you may need braces and refer you to an orthodontist. An **orthodontist** is a dentist that specializes in making sure your teeth are straight. **Braces** are medical devices that are used to straighten your teeth and can be used to correct teeth misalignments, such as crooked teeth, an **overbite** (when your top teeth stick out farther than your bottom teeth), or an **underbite** (when your bottom teeth stick out farther than your top teeth). If you sucked your thumb when you were younger, causing your top teeth to become rounded, braces could also fix this problem. The most common forms of braces are:

- ♥ **Metal braces:** Stainless steel brackets and wires

- ♥ **Ceramic braces:** Clear or tooth-colored brackets and wires

- ♥ **Clear aligners:** Transparent hard plastic inserts that are placed over your teeth

Your orthodontist will examine your teeth and determine which types of braces are best for your teeth.

WHAT HAPPENS IF I NEED BRACES?

Look around your classroom next time you are in school. A few of your classmates probably already have braces. Having braces in your younger years is completely normal, and most kids get them. Here's what happens when you get braces:

- ♥ **Step 1:** Your orthodontist will examine your teeth by x-ray to determine how your teeth will grow (if they have not grown already).

- ♥ **Step 2:** Your teeth will be properly cleaned, and bonding glue will be placed on each tooth. Don't worry! This bonding glue is taken off at the end of your braces.

- ♥ **Step 3:** Your brackets are placed on each tooth, and the wires are placed through the brackets.

Braces are normally left on for 1–2 years, as long as you are keeping up with your doc visits and using your rubber bands correctly. **Rubber bands** are small elastic bands placed over your brackets to guide your teeth in realigning. The fun part about wearing rubber bands is that you can change the colors! Braces can be uncomfortable, and you may notice your teeth really hurt at first. Avoid eating hard food items like apples and go for a bowl of soup instead for the first few days after having your braces put on or after you have your braces tightened at the doc visits. Your orthodontist will most likely tighten your braces at each visit.

CARING FOR YOUR TEETH IN BRACES

Caring for your teeth in braces is very important! Wearing braces means that food and bacteria can become trapped easily and cause cavities. Remember, always brush your teeth at least twice a day for at least 2 minutes each time. You can even brush lightly each time after eating to make sure food and sugars are properly cleaned from your mouth. Mouthwash is also a good idea to keep in your purse or backpack to rinse in between brushing. Do not ever drink mouthwash and only use the recommended amount on the back of your bottle. Even when your teeth are sore after a tightening, you must still brush to remove any plaque buildup and food after eating.

Here are a few foods you want to avoid while wearing braces:

- Gum
- Popcorn
- Chewy bread
- Sticky and crunchy candy
- Hard foods like apples and carrots

!Pop Quiz!

Have you been paying attention? Let's review what we have learned so far.

1. What are the signs that I may need glasses or contacts?

_____

_____

_____

2. What are some ways that I can protect my vision?

_____

_____

_____

3. What are eardrums?

   a. A type of musical instrument
   b. The vibrating membranes inside of your ears that respond to incoming sound waves
   c. The name of a cool new rock band

4. What are 3 ways to protect your ears when wearing headphones?

   a. _____

   b. _____

   c. _____

5.   What are the 6 steps to brushing your teeth?

   a. _____

   b. _____

   c. _____

   d. _____

   e. _____

   f. _____

6.   What are braces?

   a.   Something that you put on your head to make sure
        your hair stays in place
   b.   Medical devices that are used to straighten your
        teeth and can be used to correct teeth misalignment
   c.   A cage to put my pet in so they don't escape!

7.   How long are braces typically worn?

   a.   1–2 years
   b.   10 years
   c.   5 years

8.   What foods should I avoid when wearing braces?
     List all 5.

   a. _____

   b. _____

   c. _____

   d. _____

   e. _____

The Girl's Guide to Puberty

DAILY CHECK-IN & SELF-LOVE AFFIRMATIONS

SCRUB-A-DUB-DUB: HOW TO CLEAN YOUR BODY

What do rocks use for personal hygiene?
Geodorant! (Get it? Because geodes are a
type of rock!)

Okay, you may not think my jokes are funny, but c'mon, there aren't too many jokes about personal hygiene! **Personal hygiene** refers to how you care for and clean your body. And going through puberty means that you are going to notice a *lot* of changes. Let's explore a few of these changes together.

IS IT HOT IN HERE OR IS IT ME?

Have you noticed that your body feels wet in certain areas all of a sudden? That's because, during puberty, those crazy hormones are making your sweat glands a lot more active than they've ever been before! **Sweat glands** are small tubular structures on the skin that produce sweat. The act of sweating is called **perspiration**, not to be confused with precipitation, which is what happens when it rains. Sweat glands are kind of like pores, but they don't cause pimples. Instead, they produce sweat, which can happen when you are hot, nervous, anxious, or really from anything at all...and you may start to notice a little thing called body odor. **Body odor** is a big term that covers all the smells that come from your body. Body odor doesn't have to be a bad thing, but when it comes to sweat, it can be an offensive smell instead of a sweet one.

WHAT MAKES SWEAT SO STINKY?

Sweat contains a lot of bad bacteria, waste, and toxins from inside your body. **Toxins** are harmful substances in the body that come from food, sugars, and other things. Sweating is your body's way of removing these things from inside of you, so technically, sweat is a good thing! That doesn't mean you want to smell bad because of it, nor should you have to. The most common places you may sweat and find stinky body odor are your underarms, breasts, genital area, and feet. Your hands can sweat a lot too, but they don't normally stink (they can feel clammy and sticky instead).

Using Deodorant

Deodorant is used for your armpits to prevent or mask your body odor. Only apply deodorant to clean, dry skin. Remembering to apply deodorant can be tough! Keep your deodorant in your eyesight as a reminder to use it, especially before leaving the house. You can also keep deodorant in your school locker in case you forget to apply it at home! There are many types of deodorant, from antiperspirant (which keeps you from sweating) to natural deodorants (which contain fewer chemicals and can be better for your body). Talk to your parents about which deodorant is best for you.

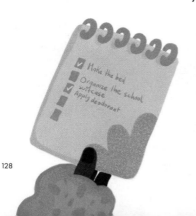

Let's learn how we can prevent stinky sweat and keep our bodies smelling fresh.

The Girl's Guide to Puberty

PROPER BATHING

If you are a kid who enjoys bath time, this section should be a lot of fun! Bathing is the number one thing you can do to prevent bad body odor and keep your skin clean. Bathing can be done in a shower or by running water in a clean bathtub. However you choose to bathe, you should do it every single day, especially on days of heavy sports, play, or activities.

How Do I Take a Bath?

- ♥ **Step 1:** Turn your water on to the desired temperature. The water should be hot but not too hot! Not only is warm water soothing, but it cleans the skin better than cold water.

- ♥ **Step 2:** Use a clean washcloth, lather it with soap, and wash your body. Take your time in each of your important areas, paying special attention to behind your ears, neck, underarms, genital area, hands, and feet. Don't forget to wash your back. You can stretch your arms behind you to wash your back or use a body sponge or scrubber with a handle to get to the hard-to-reach places.

- ♥ **Step 3:** Rinse off, repeat, and wash one more time to make sure you are properly cleaned.

HOW YOU WASH IS IMPORTANT TOO!

Bathing is not created equal, meaning how you bathe and what products you use when bathing matter. Let's start with your products.

- ♥ **Soap:** Your body soap can be in liquid or bar form. Choose a gentle and natural cleanser that does not contain a lot of fragrances and perfume to avoid body irritation. You should never use scented soap on your vaginal area.

- ♥ **Bubble bath:** Bubble bath is used for relaxing baths. Make sure to choose a bubble bath that does not contain a lot of fragrance or perfumes. Even though it may smell great, it can cause irritation of the skin, especially in your vaginal area.

♥ **Bath oils:** Bath oils can be added to your bath water for relaxation, to add a nice fragrance to your bath, and soften rough or dry skin. Do not use more than the recommended amount (normally only a few drops), as bath oil can clog the drain. Ask your parents before using.

♥ **Washcloth:** Make sure you use a washcloth when bathing to gently rub the skin. Do not scrub your skin too hard. A washcloth helps lift the dirt so that it rinses off easily. Washcloths should only be used once or twice before being replaced with a clean washcloth to not transfer bacteria after bathing.

♥ **Exfoliator: Exfoliation** is the process of removing dead skin, dirt, and bacteria from the body with a grainy substance or cloth. Exfoliators can be a body scrub, soap scrub, or a washcloth. You should not start exfoliating until your teen years, and this should only be done on a weekly basis instead of with every bath. If you are using a body scrub, make sure that you first soften the skin by taking a warm bath or shower, rinsing off the soap, and then applying your exfoliator. Use your hands to gently rub the exfoliator in a circular motion, and then rinse off. If you are using an exfoliating washcloth, soften the skin first with a regular washcloth and bathe, then use your exfoliating washcloth with soap and warm water.

♥ **Foot pumice stone:** You can use a foot pumice stone in the shower to gently remove dead skin from the bottom of your feet. You should not use foot pumice stones until your teen years. Be very careful not to scrub too hard or too long and not break the skin when using pumice stones. Make sure your feet are softened first by having them in the water for at least 5 minutes before using your stone. Make sure to wash your pumice stone after each use with soap and water, replacing your pumice stone once a month. You should only use your pumice stone once a week.

♥ **Bath towels:** Only use a clean bath towel to dry off your skin. Pat dry your skin instead of rubbing it dry. Bath towels should only be used once or twice before being replaced. This is to not transfer dirty bacteria to clean skin. Make sure you are using a separate bath towel for your body and your hair. Your hair shampoos and conditioners can contain ingredients that can irritate the skin and cause breakouts.

♥ **Body oil and lotion:** It is important to restore moisture to your skin after bathing. Dry skin tends to crack, which can be itchy and uncomfortable. If you are using body oil, apply a small amount to all parts of your body while your skin is still damp so that the oil **absorbs** or soaks into the skin. Since body lotion can be thicker, you can apply this to completely dry skin.

DOES IT MATTER HOW I BATHE MY BODY?

Absolutely! A general rule of thumb? Start with your important parts first. It may seem silly to wash your hands in the bath, but before cleaning your body, wash your hands first! Even though they will be covered with soap while you are bathing, take the time to wash your hands by scrubbing between your fingers and gently rubbing under your nails. Wash your hands for at least 20 seconds.

After you have washed your hands, wash your face. Since you are using your clean hands to wash your face, you should wash your face first with your fingers or washcloth before using your washcloth on other parts of your body. You may even keep a washcloth in your bath that is only used for your face. If you are taking a bath instead of a shower, it's a good idea to wash your face first since the water is the cleanest when you first get into the bathtub. A gentle reminder: if you are taking a sit-down bath to soak and relax, a quick shower to rinse off afterward can remove any leftover dirt from your body.

Clean your vaginal area next. Your vaginal area is one of the most sensitive parts of your entire body. You want to avoid washing your vaginal area after cleaning other parts of your body that may contain more dirt and bacteria. Always use a clean washcloth or your clean hands to wash your vagina. We will discuss how to keep your vagina clean next.

After washing your important parts, you can start bathing your other important parts! Don't forget to pay a little more attention to your underarms and feet. Wash your feet just like you wash your hands. Scrub between your toes, gently under your nails, and the soles of your feet. Sit down or lean against the bathroom wall to prevent slipping and falling when cleaning your feet.

HOW TO KEEP YOUR VULVA CLEAN

Let's start with the basics when it comes to vaginal care. When it comes to keeping your vulva clean, it starts long before your bath. The first step to a clean vulva is making sure that you wipe properly every time you use the restroom. What is the proper way to wipe? Wipe from front to back. Start at the top of your vulva (right at the clitoris) and do a single wipe all the way down, ending at your anus. Never use the same tissue to re-wipe the vulva unless you are folding the tissue over for a clean side. Urinating tends to splash, so make sure you are wiping the outside of your vulva too. Never put tissue inside of your vulval canal. Also, avoid wiping too hard. It doesn't take much! Just a soft and gentle swoop will wipe your pee away!

If you have done more than pee, ahem...gone number 2, you still want to first wipe front to back and if you need a little extra attention to clean your backside, use a clean tissue and wipe starting at your anus and right above your anus (toward your back). You don't want to wipe back to front—your anus toward your vaginal canal—because your anus is for waste removal, which contains a lot of bacteria. Wiping waste toward your vaginal canal can cause vulval infections and a bad odor. You can also ask your parents to buy wet cloths for wiping, which are safe for flushing. When using a wet cloth, follow up gently with a tissue, patting your vulva to make sure all wetness is gone. A wet vulva can also cause odor, irritation, and infection.

Always wash your hands after using the restroom.

How to Wash Your Vulva During Your Bath

Cleaning your vulva is not like cleaning any other parts of your body. Your vulva is special and should be handled with care! Here's how to wash your vulva:

♥ **Step 1:** Use an unscented soap. Using your clean hands or a clean washcloth, start at the top of your mons pubis (where the hair grows!) and gently rub the area clean, taking your hands in between your legs and rubbing softly back and forth. Rinse your hands, washcloth, and outer vagina area.

- ♥ **Step 2:** Spread the **labia**, or lips of your vulva, and, using only warm water, wash your vulva and clitoris. Never use soap inside of your vaginal canal. Your vaginal canal is a self-cleaning part of your body, meaning that it produces its own natural cleaning elements to stay healthy. Using soap inside of your vaginal canal can cause irritation and infection. Always be gentle! Your skin is very thin on your vulva, and if you rub too hard, you can cause a vaginal tear, which hurts and can be uncomfortable.

- ♥ **Step 3:** Wash your anus with a mild soap and washcloth. Do not rub too hard to prevent tearing. Gentle circular motions work best! It is best to wash your anus after you have cleaned all other parts of your body.

- ♥ **Step 4:** Finish bathing (remember to clean your anus last!) and dry off. Do not rub your vulva when drying off. Instead, pat with your towel to make sure it is dry.

Underwear Care

After bathing, put on clean underwear. Cotton panties are best! Cotton underwear is breathable and absorbs wetness. This helps to prevent vaginal infections. Change your underwear every day and avoid wearing the same pair of panties for more than 24 hours.

How to Detect a Vaginal Infection

A **vaginal infection** is a condition that causes your vagina to become inflamed and irritated. Vaginal infections can be very common as you are learning how to properly care for your private area. Every person with a vulva has had a vaginal infection at least once or twice in their lifetime! Getting a vaginal infection does not mean you are dirty or anything is wrong with you. These are easy to treat and can be prevented with proper washing. Here are some ways that you can determine if you have a vaginal infection:

- ♥ You experience a burning sensation when urinating.

- ♥ Your vulva feels hot and uncomfortable when you walk.

- ♥ You are producing abnormal discharge that is thick and white or discolored—yellow, green, or gray.

- ♥ You notice a bad vaginal odor.

If you notice any of these signs, talk to one of your parents about your symptoms, and if necessary, a doctor's visit may be advised for medication. Most times, vaginal infections can be cured with over-the-counter medication, natural herbs, and better cleaning habits.

♥ **Yeast infection:** These infections happen when too much yeast is produced inside of your vaginal canal. This can be due to overactive hormones, not properly drying your vulva, or the foods that you eat. Signs of a yeast infection are **inflammation** (or burning sensation) inside your vulva and/or vaginal canal during urination; thick, cottage-cheese discharge; and vaginal itchiness.

♥ **Bacterial Vaginosis:** Your vagina grows healthy and unhealthy bacteria. When there is an imbalance in this growth, bacterial vaginosis can occur. You can also get bacterial vaginosis from using soap inside of your vaginal canal. Signs to look out for are bad "fishy" odor; thin white, gray, or green discharge; and vaginal itchiness.

Yeast infections and bacterial vaginosis are easily treated and don't last forever! Make sure to talk to a parent immediately if you think you have a vaginal infection. Avoid using perfume, scented soaps, lotions, and toilet paper on your private area. Keep your vulva healthy by practicing good cleaning habits.

!Pop Quiz!

Have you been paying attention? Let's review what we've learned so far.

1. What is perspiration?

    a. What happens when rain falls
    b. Sweating from my body
    c. The sweat glands on my skin

2. What are the 3 proper steps to taking a bath?

    a. _____

    b. _____

    c. _____

3. In what order should I bathe my body?

    a. Legs, arms, face, vulva
    b. Feet, face, vulva, back
    c. Hands, face, vulva, body, anus

4. How often should I change my washcloth and bath towel?

    a. Once a month
    b. Once a week
    c. After 1 or 2 uses

5. True or False: When wiping my vulva, I should wipe gently from front to back.

    a. True
    b. False

6. What are the 4 steps to cleaning my vulva?

    a. _____

    b. _____

    c. _____

    d. _____

7. What are the 2 types of vaginal infections?

    a. _____

    b. _____

DAILY CHECK-IN & SELF-LOVE AFFIRMATIONS

MY BODY IS DIFFERENT. IS THAT NORMAL?

You have probably never noticed your body as much before starting puberty and your period. As your body begins to go through its unique changes, your self-awareness may peak. At the beginning of your journal, we talked about **self-love**, which is to put yourself first in a state of happiness and appreciation for every part of you that makes you, *You*. So, what is self-awareness? **Self-awareness** is recognizing who you are, inside and out. It means being knowledgeable about your feelings, how you respond to these feelings, and what may be triggers for you. **Triggers** are things that can bother you and change your emotional state. We will talk about emotions soon. Self-awareness is also knowing what your body looks like, especially in comparison to those around you. It is completely normal to compare yourself to others. We *all* do it! Even as adults! What is not healthy, though, is to compare yourself in a way that makes you feel less than. You are special and unique just the way you are.

The best part of being a person is that we all come in different shapes and sizes. Some of us are tall. Others are short! Some of us are a size 2, and others are a size 10! Think about it. If we were all the same, life would not be as fun. Our size, the color of our skin, and our beautiful hair texture make us different from those around us, but none of these characteristics make us any less than. As we grow, our bodies will continue to change and grow with us all the way into adulthood.

With television, social media, and comparing ourselves to friends at school, it is important to check in with yourself on how you feel about yourself. Here are some questions you can ask yourself:

What are some things I love about who I am on the inside?

_____

_____

_____

_____

_____

_____

_____

_____

_____

_____

_____

_____

What are some things I love about myself on the outside?

_____

_____

_____

_____

_____

_____

_____

_____

_____

_____

_____

_____

Who is a friend that I admire that has characteristics different from mine? What are they?

_____

_____

_____

_____

_____

_____

_____

_____

What are some things that make me special and unique?

_____

_____

_____

_____

_____

_____

_____

_____

_____

_____

_____

_____

WEIGHT GAIN & WEIGHT LOSS

Let's learn a funny-sounding new word: Fluctuation, not to be confused with flatulence! **Fluctuation** is the irregular rise and fall of a number, in this case, your weight. **Flatulence** is to release gas...or fart. It's okay to laugh! Now, back to fluctuation.

Puberty comes with plenty of new things with your body to wrap your head around. Gaining or losing weight is one of them, otherwise known as weight fluctuation. Throughout this entire journal, you have been reminded of one special fact: You are perfect just the way you are! Even still, a change in your weight during puberty can come with a lot of questions about what is normal or acceptable, just as we discussed earlier. For girls, you may notice you are gaining weight in your hips, thighs, and butt, along with your growing breasts. Why? Those wonderful little hormones are hard at work. Growth is a vital part of your life! You may also notice other girls in your class are "filling out" faster than you. This is a gentle reminder to be okay with where you are. You will have plenty of time to grow. Don't rush the process.

Watch Out For Unhealthy Signs

Weight fluctuation can cause you to become uncomfortable with your body. Even though this is normal, how you handle these emotions is important. If you are having unhealthy thoughts about your weight, please talk to a parent or trusted adult immediately. In fact, this may be a good time to discuss this portion of your journal with your parents. There are a few negative responses that can happen when you become aware of your body, called eating disorders. An **eating disorder** is when you drastically change your eating habits to obtain a different shape that is otherwise unnatural to your current body shape. Let's talk about the most common eating disorders.

- ♥ **Anorexia Nervosa:** Anorexia is the act of not eating or over-exercising to lose weight quickly. Signs to look out for are skipping meals, avoiding certain foods, and/ or an obsession with working out.

- ♥ **Bulimia Nervosa:** Bulimia is the act of overeating, or **binge eating**, followed by self-induced vomiting to lose weight.

- ♥ **Binge-Eating Disorder:** Binge eating is the act of over-eating foods, especially unhealthy meals.

All of these eating disorders are connected to **body dysmorphia** or an unhealthy view of your body image. Remember, the best way to maintain a healthy weight is with a balanced diet and moderate exercise. We will talk about how you can incorporate healthy foods and working out into your routine instead of developing eating disorders that can have lasting negative effects on your life.

If you are struggling with an eating disorder, please talk to a parent or trusted adult immediately.

!Pop Quiz!

Have you been paying attention? Let's review what we've learned so far.

1. In your own words, describe what "self-love" means.

   _____

   _____

   _____

   _____

2. In your own words, describe what "self-awareness" means.

   _____

   _____

   _____

   _____

3. What are triggers?

   a. When you point your finger at someone
   b. Things that can bother you and change your emotional state
   c. Something that you step on that sounds an alarm

4. Do you have any triggers that you can think of?
   List them below.

   a. _____

   b. _____

   c. _____

4. What is weight fluctuation?

   a. What happens when I fart!
   b. What happens when I put my dog on a scale
   c. What happens when my weight rises and falls

4. True or False: Weight fluctuation is caused by my
   hormones during puberty and it's perfectly normal.

   a. True
   b. False

3. What unhealthy signs should I look out for if I think I may
   be developing an eating disorder? (Circle all that apply.)

   a. Overeating
   b. Avoiding food
   c. Becoming obsessed with working out
   d. Making myself vomit after a meal

5. Name 3 people I feel safe talking to if I think I may be
   developing an eating disorder.

   a. _____

   b. _____

   c. _____

DAILY CHECK-IN &
SELF-LOVE AFFIRMATIONS

DID YOU KNOW THAT THERE ARE OVER 3,000 WORDS FOR EMOTIONS?

This little fact gives an entirely new meaning when someone asks you, "How are you feeling today?" doesn't it? Let's talk about your emotions and how puberty plays a part in how you really feel.

WHY AM I SO EMOTIONAL?

Growing up can feel like an emotional rollercoaster. One moment, you feel happy and the next moment, you are sad. One day you are laughing and the next you have 100 names for tears! I am sure you can guess what the cause is for these changes in emotion. Yep. *Hormones!* The hormones estrogen, progesterone, and testosterone have really complicated names but a very simple result when it comes to your emotions—to make them feel uncontrollable. These hormones are responsible for **mood swings**, which are the emotional ups and downs you may feel during puberty. Here's the good news: your emotions are controllable, even when they feel like they aren't.

LEARNING HOW TO IDENTIFY YOUR EMOTIONS

One of the first steps to controlling your emotions is learning how to identify them properly. Emotions are more than just happy, sad, or mad. There are emotional feelings such as disappointment, embarrassment, anxiousness, and jealousy. Learning how to identify emotions will help you be a better communicator with your family and friends, but most importantly, with yourself on how you are feeling. Let's explore a few scenarios where your emotions may get a better hold of you and how you can handle them.

My Sibling Won't Stay Out of My Room!

EMOTIONS: ANGER, ANNOYANCE

If you have a younger or older sibling that is bothering you, you may notice during puberty that your response to their behavior may not be nice or gentle. Instead of calling on Mom or Dad to help, you may experience an **emotional outburst** or a certain rise of emotion—in this case, anger, which makes you react immediately by yelling at them or becoming physical. Hitting and yelling are *never* the answer when dealing with conflict.

What is a better way you can handle the emotion of anger in this situation?

_____

_____

My Parents Just Don't Understand Me!

EMOTIONS: CONFUSION, FRUSTRATION

Feeling misunderstood by your parents during puberty is very normal. Your changing emotions can have you feeling very confused about yourself! It may seem like you are getting in more trouble, and your parents may even accuse you of having an "attitude problem" or **temper tantrums**, which are also emotional outbursts. When you are feeling misunderstood, it can result in you becoming quiet and **withdrawn**, meaning you are less likely to communicate with your parents about how you really feel.

What are some ways that you can communicate better with your parents when you are feeling misunderstood?

_____

_____

_____

_____

Help! I Have a Test on Monday and I Am Not Prepared.

EMOTIONS: ANXIOUSNESS, DISCOURAGEMENT, NOT FEELING SMART OR GOOD ENOUGH

School can be very hard, especially when it seems like you are not learning as quickly as those around you. When you have a test or a quiz coming up that you are not prepared for, it can make you feel **anxious**, which are feelings of uneasiness or nervousness about an upcoming event. Not feeling smart enough can also cause you to **overcompensate** or take extreme measures to show up in another way to distract those around you from the fact that you may not know something. This may look like being the class clown to make people like you or acting out in class to avoid answering a question.

What are some ways that you can express to your teacher or parent that you need help with a school subject?

_____

_____

_____

_____

_____

My Best Friend at School Is Talking about Me Behind My Back.

EMOTION: SADNESS, EMBARRASSMENT, HURT

Friend drama is very common in middle school and high school. The truth is that children and teens can be mean or become bullies. Why? Because they also experience puberty and may not have the tools or help at home to learn how to deal with negative emotions. One day, you may come to school and find out your best friend has been telling your secrets to others. Or your friend has stopped talking to you for no reason at all!

Instead of pretending that their actions do not bother you, it is important to identify what you are feeling.

Have you experienced friend betrayal? What are some ways that you handled it?

_____

_____

_____

_____

_____

If you are experiencing bullying at school, please talk to a parent or trusted adult immediately.

My Friend Gets Way More Attention Than Me and Their Clothes Are Cooler.

EMOTIONS: JEALOUSY, ENVY, UNDESERVING

Friendship jealousy can happen when it seems like your friend is getting more attention than you. Because of puberty, our bodies will all develop differently—some faster or slower than others. Feeling jealous of your friends does not mean you do not like them or want to be friends with them anymore. Learning to identify these emotions can help you avoid negative reactions toward them. Remember, you are unique and special just the way you are. Learning how to recognize what makes our friends special and unique can be a great help to our self-esteem. **Self-esteem** is confidence in how you feel about yourself. Appreciating what makes them different and special can never take away from what makes you special.

What are some ways you can avoid negative reactions when you feel jealous of your friends?

_____

_____

_____

_____

I Have a Crush on Someone Who Doesn't Like Me Back.

EMOTIONS: REJECTION, HEARTBREAK, UNWORTHINESS

With puberty comes stronger feelings of being attracted to those around you. Unfortunately, these feelings are not always returned, and it can feel like the end of the world. Here is a gentle reminder: There are people out there who will like you just the way you are. Heartbreak is a very strong emotion that can lead to feelings of unworthiness and depression. This can also happen if a relationship with someone ends. It is very important to properly identify these emotions so you can know if what you are feeling is considered normal or if additional steps of help need to be taken to avoid unnecessary sadness that can have negative effects on your life.

What are some ways that you can deal with rejection?

_____

_____

_____

_____

_____

If you are having extreme feelings of depression that make you unable to get out of bed or want to harm yourself, please talk to a parent or trusted adult immediately.

I Am Having Issues with My Self Identity. I Don't Know Who I Am.

Self-identification is the act of recognizing your potential, qualities, and how you show up in the world. When you learn that your self-identification is different from those around you, there can be extreme feelings of confusion about who you are. Self-identity defines you, and it's always a good idea to show up as who you really are. By doing this, you will find friends and social circles who are just like you.

What are some ways that you self-identify? Examples can include being a meat-eater or a vegetarian, being an athlete or an artist, or identifying your gender.

_____

_____

_____

_____

_____

If you are struggling with self-identity issues, please speak to a parent or trusted adult immediately.

HEALTHY WAYS TO TACKLE YOUR EMOTIONS

Let's make one thing clear: *Emotions are healthy!* Even the ones that don't always feel good. **Emotions** are your mind's mental response to outward or inward elements. Learning to identify, control, and express your emotions is a part of your growing experience. So don't beat yourself up if you don't always get it right. Let's cover a few healthy ways that you can tackle your emotions.

♥ **Meditation or prayer:** Depending on your religious beliefs or background, praying and/or meditating can be a healthy response to emotions. Try this: Close your eyes and count backward from ten. Try to quiet your thoughts and think positive thoughts or don't think about anything at all. This is a form of meditation. If you believe in God or a higher power, you can also say a prayer, asking for guidance on how to handle how you feel at that moment.

♥ **Breathing exercises:** One of the best ways to calm down is to control your breath. Take deep breaths in through your nose and blow out through your mouth. You can do this until you feel your heart rate start to slow and return to normal.

♥ **Positive self-talk:** You may notice a little voice in your head that speaks to you. This is called your subconscious. At times, your subconscious can provide negative self-talk and tell you that you are not good enough or you should not try to do something that is hard. Learn to train your subconscious to give you positive self-talk instead! When that little voice tries to tell you that you can't, tell yourself that you can! You can also remember your affirmations and repeat them to yourself to boost your emotional energy.

♥ **Write it out:** Keeping a journal or diary is a great way to express how you feel before you tell someone else how you feel. You have gotten quite a bit of practice using your journal here! A gentle reminder: your Daily Check-In and Self-Love Affirmation pages are a safe space to express your emotions right here in this book. When you repeat your affirmations, try saying them in the mirror so you can remember just how awesome you are. You can also use letter writing to express how you feel to a family or friend who has affected your mood. Sometimes it is easier to write a letter than have a conversation.

♥ **Talk it out:** Once you feel that you are in a healthy space to express how you feel, try talking through your emotions with your parents, friends, or a school counselor. This will help those around you understand how you feel and mend any uncomfortable experiences you may be having together.

♥ **Sweat it out:** Sometimes going on a run or finding a healthy way to exercise can clear your mind too! Finding a way to release pent-up emotions in a healthy way is always a great idea!

WHEN TO SEEK IMMEDIATE HELP

If your emotions ever feel out of your control, please seek help from your parents, a teacher, a school counselor, or another trusted adult. Not being able to control every single emotion is nothing to be ashamed of. We all need a little help now and again. Some signs to look out for are:

- ♥ You find yourself crying uncontrollably for no reason at all.

- ♥ You are experiencing extreme emotional ups and downs that affect your daily routine.

- ♥ You have thoughts of harming yourself or others.

Remember, your parents and teachers are here to help you. You don't have to go through anything alone.

!Pop Quiz!

Have you been paying attention? Let's review what we've learned so far!

1. What are emotions?

    a. Your mind's mental response to outward or inward elements
    b. Your physical response to a situation
    c. One of your 5 senses

2. Name 5 happy emotions that you can feel:

    a. _____

    b. _____

    c. _____

    d. _____

    e. _____

3. What are 5 healthy ways to tackle my emotions?

    a. _____

    b. _____

    c. _____

    d. _____

    e. _____

4. What signs should I look out for that I may need help when dealing with my emotions? (Circle all that apply.)

   a. I have extreme emotional ups and downs.
   b. I can calm myself down on my own when experiencing anger.
   c. I have thoughts of self-harm or of harming someone else.
   d. I can feel better after writing in my journal.
   e. I cry unexpectedly for no reason at all.

5. List 3 people in your personal life that you feel safe enough to talk to about your emotions.

   1. _____

   2. _____

   3. _____

6. True or False: Emotions, both good and bad, are completely healthy!

   a. True
   b. False

DAILY CHECK-IN &
SELF-LOVE AFFIRMATIONS

MEAT, FISH
EGGS

AND DAIRY PRODUCTS

MILK

VEGETABLE

FRUIT

GRAINS

G

MAKING HEALTHY CHOICES

As you get older, you will learn that life is all about making healthy choices. Whether the choice is what you eat, working out, or making good decisions, one of the most important lessons you can learn is accountability. **Accountability** is being personally responsible for the decisions that you make in your life. It's true—you are growing up! While your parents or trusted guardians are still responsible for you, you are also responsible for You. Let's review a few healthy choices that you can take accountability for.

YOU ARE WHAT YOU EAT

Choosing Foods That Fuel Your Body

Healthy foods are essential to growing a healthy body. As you have learned in your journal, your body is doing some pretty amazing and *big* things to help you grow. The best way to reward all of your body's hard work is by recharging with food that will keep your bones healthy, skin glowing, and muscles strong. Below are two food pyramids: one for meat and dairy eaters and one for vegans and vegetarians.

Food Pyramids

Meat, fish, eggs: 2 servings
Milk and dairy products: 2 servings
Veggies: 3 servings
Fruit: 2 servings
Grains: 6 servings

You are still a kid! Have fun with your nutrition! Whether you are a meat-eater or vegetarian, here are a few tips on keeping a balanced diet:

- ♥ It's *always* a good idea to drink lots of water. Instead of chugging water once or twice, drink it moderately, meaning drinking throughout the day. Rule of thumb: Try to drink at least 8 glasses of water each day.

Juices and soda may seem tasty but are not great for your skin. Try sweetening your water with fruits and veggies instead.

♥ You don't have to give up sweets to be healthy. Eat your sugars and treats sparingly. Consider them a reward after a long week versus a daily snack.

  There are a *lot* of veggies out there. Don't get too down on yourself if you're not a fan of spinach. You can try veggies like broccoli, salad, leafy greens, okra, and carrots too!

 If veggies are hard to stomach, try drinking your nutrition as smoothies or green juices. You can mix in fruit to sweeten the taste. Make sure you ask an adult for help before using a blender.

♥ Limit your number of fried foods. Opt for grilled or baked foods instead.

How Food Affects Your Body

It may help you decide to make healthier food choices if you know how they affect your body. Remember those pesky little hormones? What you eat really influences how they affect you as well. Here's a cool fact: *all* living things, including plants, have hormones. And because you already have your own, you want to stay away from certain foods that contain too many additional hormones. A few foods that can disrupt your hormones during puberty are:

♥ Soy-based foods
♥ Very salty foods like chips
♥ "Junk" foods like burgers, pizzas, and fried foods

The Girl's Guide to Puberty

♥ Processed foods
♥ Soft drinks and non-organic pre-packaged juices

The key thing to remember is moderation. **Moderation** just means avoiding extremes. You can enjoy all these things sometimes, just not all the time.

FOOD AND YOUR SKIN

Puberty causes acne. Acne can also be caused by an unhealthy diet. Puberty plus an unhealthy diet is a breeding ground for excessive acne! Sugary foods and highly acidic drinks are major factors in breakouts. Oh, and chocolate. Our beloved chocolate, which you may crave right before your period, can actually cause you to break out more. Write out a few healthy alternatives for unhealthy snacks:

Instead of a Snickers bar, I can have _____.

Instead of dairy ice cream, I'll make _____
ice cream with real fruit!

No sodas for me! I will use these 3 fruits and veggies to sweeten my water:

1. _____

2. _____

3. _____

There's this little thing called bloating that can occur right before menstruation. **Bloating** is what happens when your gastrointestinal (GI) tract fills with air and gas, causing your lower belly to pudge more than it should. Bloating can create a lot of insecurity around your body image and self-esteem. I'm here to tell you, everybody bloats! While your period can cause bloating, your food and eating habits can also affect your body. Even though bloating is completely natural, you can avoid certain foods that can make you bloat more.

A few ways to avoid bloating are:

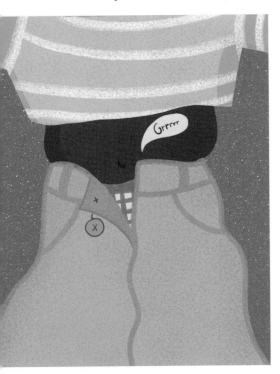

- Eat slowly! Try not to rush your meals. Instead, chew your food completely before swallowing for easy digestion.

- Avoid foods that give you gas—food like sodas full of carbonation, dairy, and even chewing gum! Remember, moderation is key here.

MAKING THE HEALTHY CHOICE TO EXERCISE

Working out can be a lot of fun! Even though you probably feel *too old* to want to play on the playground, running around with your friends at the park when you were younger was a healthy exercise for you, and it's important to maintain that level of activity through your tween and teen years.

Think of it like this: We have 24 hours in a day. Can you commit to one hour each day of moving your body?

Working out can be:

- ♥ Jogging
- ♥ Riding your bike
- ♥ Sports
- ♥ Dancing
- ♥ Horseback riding
- ♥ Playing with your pets outside
- ♥ And yes, playing at the park! You are not *too old*!

Practice Safety When Working Out

You can incorporate some safe practices into your workout routine. Here are a few:

- ♥ **Drink lots of water:** Working out can make you sweat! Sweating is good for you because it helps to detox the body, but you must replenish what comes out. Make sure that you are staying properly hydrated before, during, and after your workout activity.

- ♥ **Stretch first:** Working out causes your muscles to stretch and grow. Before jumping into your exercise, practice some light stretching to warm up the muscles, and once finishing your exercise, cool down with a few stretches as well. Proper stretching is key. Don't rush or overdo it. Stretch your body slowly and gently while breathing properly in between. Consider these stretches: toe touches, side bends, and stretching your arms above your head as sufficient warm-up stretches before and after workouts.

- ♥ **Don't overdo it:** Working out faster, longer, or lifting more than you are able will not help you to get in shape faster. Instead, this can actually cause burnout or, even worse, injury. **Burnout** happens when you overextend yourself and are only able to maintain activity for a short amount of time. Injury can occur from overstretching the muscle, causing a tear, which results in extreme pain and soreness. Be gentle with your body and go at a safe and supportive pace.

- ♥ **Keep a healthy mindset:** Your mindset is the most important safety practice when working out. With your changing body, make sure that you are staying positive with your workout—remembering that you are working out for your overall health and not to see drastic and unhealthy results. You are perfect just the way you are. If you are experiencing body insecurities that are causing you to exercise more than you should, please talk to a trusted adult.

♥ **Work out with your friends and family:**
Exercising with friends and family can be great motivation for staying in shape and bonding together! Grab a few friends and enjoy a jog around the neighborhood. Working out in groups also keeps you accountable and consistent with your exercise routine.

!Pop Quiz!

Have you been paying attention?
Let's review what we've learned so far!

1. According to your food pyramid, what is the right number of servings of veggies you should have every day?

   a. 5 servings
   b. 3 servings
   c. 7 servings

2. Name 3 veggies that you love to eat!

   a. _____

   b. _____

   c. _____

3. How many glasses of water should you drink in a day?

   a. 4 glasses
   b. 8 glasses
   c. 2 glasses

4. What are 3 activities that I can do that can be considered exercise?

   a. _____

   b. _____

   c. _____

5. What are the 5 safety practices I should do when working out?

   a. _____

   b. _____

   c. _____

   d. _____

   e. _____

MAKING THE HEALTHY CHOICE TO REST

With the world happening all around you—new thoughts, friendships, and activities—rest may feel like the very last thing that you want to do. But a good night's sleep is essential to your body and brain's development. Resting well improves your mental health, memory, concentration, and **immune system,** which keeps you healthy, helps to improve your mood, and even gives you a better metabolism! **Metabolism** is your body's chemical response to digesting food and turning it into energy. Doctor's orders: It is recommended to have 8 to 10 hours every night. How can you maintain healthy rest?

- ♥ **Create a nighttime ritual:** Making a schedule for rest can improve your chances of getting quality ZZZs. If your bedtime is at 9:00 p.m. every night, try to start your sleep schedule an hour earlier. This can include your bath, brushing your teeth, a cup of warm tea, reading a book, and journaling about your day!

- ♥ **Do not disturb:** Even though you may want to chat with your friends throughout the day, turning your phone off at night and sleeping with it away from your bed can increase your rest as well. Save mindless internet scrolling for another time besides bedtime.

- ♥ **Watch what you eat and drink:** Sugary foods and caffeinated drinks can keep you up at night. Instead of sodas and snacks, opt for a glass of water, warm milk, or tea instead. Warm drinks work to soothe your belly before bedtime and help you to relax at the end of a long day.

The Girl's Guide to Puberty

- 💜 **Listen to your body:** Napping after school or on weekends is a great habit to form. Napping in class is not. If you are feeling tired throughout the day and it's causing you to fall asleep in class, this may mean that you need to get more ZZZs at nighttime. You can also rest for a 20-minute nap during the day after school and sports for a quick recharge. Sleeping longer than 20 minutes can disrupt your nighttime sleep schedule so try and keep your naps to a minimum.

Are You Having Trouble Sleeping?

If you have a lot on your mind, a big test, or friendship drama happening at school, going to sleep at night can feel impossible. Try relaxation techniques like meditation or listening to calming music before bedtime. If you need to sleep with a nightlight for a good rest, go for it! Even adults sleep with a little light from time to time.

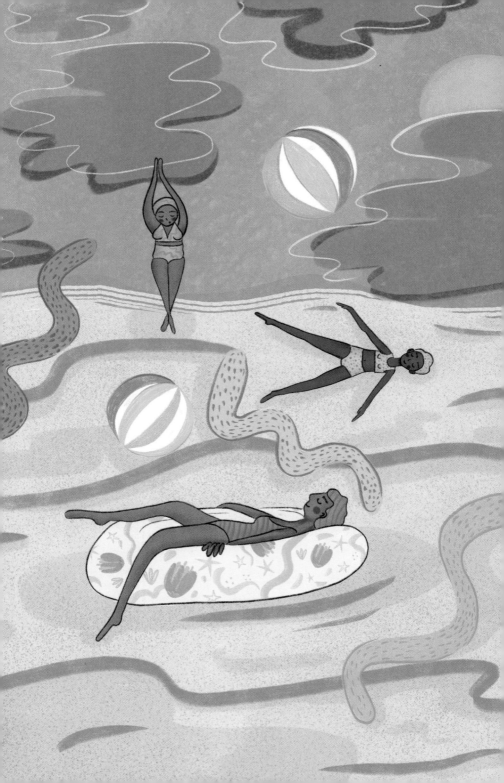

MAKING HEALTHY CHOICES IN THE COMPANY YOU KEEP

As you continue to grow, you are going to be faced with lots of new decisions to make for your life. These can be choices about your body, your friendship circles in and out of school, and your choices to be a good person. **Peer pressure** happens when people in your same age group want you to make choices that you may or may not be ready for. Peer pressure normally does not include decisions that your parents may know about right away, so it is up to you to make healthy choices in your life, even when you are away from home.

Growing up should be a fun and exciting new experience! Every day, you will face a new joy and maybe even a new challenge. Throughout the pages of your journal, you have learned a lot of new information. Even though you are here, at the end of your journal, it doesn't mean you can't use this book as a reference guide to review, reread, and rediscover all the new parts of you!

Remember, you are responsible for how you show up in this world. Make choices that make you proud. Have fun with your life and know that you are unique and special just the way you are!

* * *

Let's close out our journal with one final !Pop Quiz! to review some of the important topics discussed in this book. You will also have additional affirmation journaling pages that you can use to jot down notes, thoughts, and feelings, even after you have finished reading your journal.

Hey, you. Yes, you, reading your journal. People just like you make the world go round. Those around you love you and are so grateful for the special person that you are. Growing up is one of the best things that you can do!

The Girl's Guide to Puberty

DAILY CHECK-IN &
SELF-LOVE AFFIRMATIONS

!THE BIG POP QUIZ!

Have you been paying attention? Let's review *all* of what you've learned so far! (Refer to the pages in your journal if you need help!)

1. True or false. **Self-love** means putting yourself first in a state of happiness and appreciation for every part of you that makes you, *You*. (page 16) _____

2. What is puberty? (page 19)

   a. What happens on every full moon
   b. A special time in your life when your body (inside and out!) and emotions change
   c. A changing time in life that only girls go through

3. What are the 5 stages of puberty? (page 20)

   a. _____

   b. _____

   c. _____

   d. _____

   e. _____

4. What are 3 reasons why I may develop acne during puberty? (page 54)

a. _____

b. _____

c. _____

5. What is a period (menstruation)? (page 66)

a. The dot at the end of a sentence
b. Something that happens when I ride my bike
c. The shedding of your uterine lining of blood and tissue

6. In your own words, what are the 4 steps to cleaning your vulva? (page 135-136)

a. _____

b. _____

c. _____

d. _____

7. What are 6 ways that I can tackle my emotions? (page 164-165)

a. _____

b. _____

c. _____

d. _____

e. _____

f. _____

8. What foods should I eat or drink in moderation to stay healthy? Circle all that apply. (page 174-175)

   a. Pizza
   b. Vegetables
   c. Juices and sodas
   d. Sweets
   e. Water

9. In your own words, explain why it is healthy to keep a positive mindset when working out. (page 178-179)

   _____

   _____

   _____

   _____

10. How many hours of sleep should I get every night? (page 182)

   a. 4 hours
   b. 8 hours
   c. 2 hours

GLOSSARY

Definitions of the New Vocabulary Words
You've Learned in Your Journal!

Accountability: Being personally responsible for the decisions that you make in your life.

Acne: Bumps that may appear on your face and body.

Affirm: To make a [positive] statement in support of a person, belief system, or idea.

Affirmations: Positive statements about yourself.

Anorexia nervosa: The act of not eating or over-exercising to lose weight quickly. Signs to look out for are skipping meals, avoiding certain foods, and/or an obsession with working out.

Anus/rectum: The muscular canal from which waste leaves your body.

Anxious: Feelings of uneasiness or nervousness about an upcoming event.

Areola: The dark-pigmented circular skin that surrounds your nipple.

Bacterial vaginosis: Your vagina grows healthy and unhealthy bacteria. When there is an imbalance in this growth, bacterial vaginosis can occur. You can also get bacterial vaginosis from using soap inside the vagina. Signs to look out for are bad "fishy" odor; thin white, gray, or green discharge; and vaginal itchiness.

Binge-eating disorder: The act of overeating foods, especially unhealthy meals.

Blackheads: Blackheads are the result of open comedones. Unlike whiteheads, your pores are open and filled with oil and bacteria, resulting in black dots or bumps on your skin. Instead of your skin lacking oxygen, blackheads are caused when the open oil-filled pores receive too much oxygen. This is a process called oxidation.

Bloating: What happens when your gastrointestinal (GI) tract fills with air and gas, making your lower belly pudge more than it should.

Blush: Makeup that goes on your cheeks to give them a rosy look.

Body dysmorphia: An unhealthy view of your body image.

Body odor: A big term that covers all the smells that come from your body.

Breast tissue: milk ducts, and supportive tissue that make up your breasts.

Budding: What happens when your breasts begin to develop. Breast budding is one of the first signs of puberty.

Bulimia nervosa: The act of overeating, or binge eating, followed by self-induced vomiting to lose weight.

Burnout: Happens when you overextend yourself and can only maintain activity for a short amount of time.

Cavities: Rotten holes in your teeth caused by sugar, bacteria, candy, and sodas/juices.

Ceramic braces: Clear or tooth-colored brackets and wires.

Cervix: A canal right below your uterus that connects the uterus to the vagina.

Clear aligners: Transparent hard plastic inserts that are placed over your teeth.

Clitoris: The pear-shaped organ located right below the top of your vagina.

Combination skin: Both oily and dry skin, varies on your T-zone. Example: You may have a very dry T-zone but oily cheeks.

Complexion: Skin color.

Contacts: Small and flimsy round lenses inserted directly into your eyes to help you see.

Dandruff: Dry, itchy, and flaky skin that can lie on top of your scalp.

Dehydration: Lack of water.

Deodorant: Used for your armpits to prevent or mask your body odor.

Dermatologist: A doctor who specializes in the treatment of your hair, skin, and nails.

Dry skin: When your skin feels tight, especially after washing.

Eardrums: The vibrating membranes inside your ears that respond to incoming sound waves.

Earwax: The protective yellow waxy substance secreted in the passage of the outer ears.

Eating disorder: When you drastically change your eating habits to obtain a different shape that is otherwise unnatural to your current body shape.

Emotional outburst: A certain rise of emotion.

Emotions: Your mind's mental response to outward or inward elements.

Enamel: The thin outer covering of your teeth.

Exfoliation: The process of removing dead skin, dirt, and bacteria from the body with a grainy substance or cloth.

Eye exam: A series of tests to check your vision.

Eyeliner: A liquid or pencil form of makeup applied on top of your eyelid behind your eyelashes to give your eyes a more defined look.

Eyeshadow: A colorful powder that goes on top of your eyelids.

Fallopian tubes: The pair of tubes in which the eggs travel to the uterus.

Farsighted: Seeing objects well far away but not up close.

Fatigue: A really fancy word for feeling tired.

Feminine hygiene products: Products made especially for when you get your period.

Fertilization: The act or process of growing an egg in reproduction.

Flatulence: To release gas...or fart.

Fluctuation: The irregular rise and fall of a number.

Food cravings: The urge to eat specific foods.

Foundation: A liquid or powdered form of makeup that matches your skin to even out your skin tone and covers any breakouts.

Genitalia: An overall term for your outer sexual and reproductive organs.

Gingivitis: Gum disease that causes swollen, red, and inflamed gums.

Growth spurt: To become taller in a short period of time.

Hair follicle: The shaft opening in which the hair grows through the skin.

Hair texture: The feel and appearance of your hair.

Halitosis: Bad breath not caused by poor dental habits.

Indication: The sign of something changing.

Ingrown hairs: When the hair grows under the skin in the wrong direction, resulting in a dark or painful red bump on the skin.

Labia Majora: The outer "lips" of the opening of your vagina.

Labia Minora: The inner "lips" of the opening of your vagina.

Lice: Small parasitic insects that live on the scalp and live on blood.

Lip gloss/Chapstick: An oil that is applied to the lips for moisturization, shine, or color.

Mascara: Liquid makeup that goes on top of your eyelashes to make them darker and easier to see.

Mature: To get older.

Melanin (melanated): A darker skin color.

Menstrual cramping: A throbbing or rumbling pain that can happen in your belly and lower back.

Menstruation (period): The shedding of your uterine lining of blood and tissue.

Metal braces: Stainless steel brackets and wires.

Moderation: To avoid extremes.

Mood swings: Emotional ups and downs.

Navigate: To explore.

Nearsighted: Seeing objects up close well but not far away.

Nipple: The pointy dark part of your areola that is raised.

Normal skin: "Normal" skin simply means that your skin is neither oily nor dry. All skin is completely normal—this just refers to your balance of oils.

Oily skin: When your skin feels oily to the touch. Your fingers may be shiny when you touch your face.

Optometrist: An eye doctor.

Oral hygiene: The practice of keeping your mouth clean.

Orthodontist: A dentist that specializes in making sure your teeth are straight.

Ovaries: The female reproductive organs that produce eggs. These eggs can produce babies.

Overbite: When your top teeth stick out farther than your bottom teeth.

Overcompensate: To take extreme measures to show up in another way, to distract those around you from the fact that you may not know something.

Pads: A rectangular product made from absorbent material that is placed in the crotch of your underwear. The bottom of the pad is sticky, and the sides have wings (or flaps) that go around the bottom part of your panties to make sure the pad stays in place.

Panty liners: Thinner and smaller pads that are not as absorbent.

Period kit: A little goodie bag of items that have all the necessary things that you need to face your first period with confidence.

Period Party: An intimate celebration that celebrates a young girl getting her menstrual cycle.

Period underwear: Underwear with an absorbent material built into the crotch of your panties or a pocket to insert a pad that allows your blood flow to be caught once it is released.

Personal hygiene: Refers to how you care for and clean your body.

Perspiration: The act of sweating.

Pheromones: Your body's natural odor through your sweat glands.

Pimples: This is an umbrella term normally used for acne bumps on the body. Pimples can be sore to the touch and red on the skin. They are usually small and like to travel in clusters (or groups). Chances are if you see one pimple, a few more will be joining them soon. Pimples may have a white pus-filled tip.

Plaque buildup: A sticky film of bacteria that forms across the teeth.

PMS: Premenstrual syndrome.

Pores: Teeny tiny oil-releasing openings on your face.

Precipitation: What happens when it rains.

Primer: A lotion that you apply to the skin that acts as a barrier between your skin and makeup.

Prompt: Conversation starters.

Puberty: A special time in life when your body (inside and out!) and emotions change.

Pubic area: The V-shaped lower part of your belly right above your private part.

Pubic hair: The hair that grows on top of your vagina.

Race: The color of your skin as it relates to skin and hair texture.

Reproductive system: The tissues, glands, and organs involved in producing children.

Rite of passage: A unique experience that defines an important event in life.

Rubber bands: Small elastic bands placed over your brackets to guide your teeth in realigning.

Safe space: A space where you are allowed to be as inquisitive (curious) as you like while exploring and being honest about how this all feels for you.

Sebum: Natural oils produced by your body.

Self-awareness: Recognizing who you are, inside and out.

Self-esteem: The confidence in how you feel about yourself.

Self-identification: The act of recognizing your potential, qualities, and how you show up in the world.

Self-love: To put yourself first in a state of happiness and appreciation for every part of you that makes you, *You.*

Sensitive skin: Skin that is easily irritated by products or stress. This skin type can be oily or dry, but most commonly, sensitive skin is dry, patchy, and appears red or swollen during an irritation.

Shaving: Involves using a razor pressed up against the skin to cut the hair down to the skin.

Solution: Contact lens cleaner.

Sound waves: Moving and vibrating energy, which vibrates the eardrum.

Sperm: A male's reproductive cells.

SPF: Sun protection factor.

Sweat glands: Small tubular structures on the skin that produce sweat.

Symptoms: Groups of changes that happen together to indicate an outcome.

T-zone: The area of your face that includes your central facial features, including your forehead, nose, and chin.

Tampon: A small, cylinder feminine hygiene product inserted inside the vagina to catch blood flow.

Temper tantrums: Sudden emotional outbursts.

Toner: A skin-balancing lotion or liquid.

Toxic shock syndrome: Caused by a bacterial infection that can result in fever, vomiting, and a rash.

Toxins: The harmful substances in the body that come from food, sugars, and other things.

Training bra: Bras for young girls just starting to develop breasts.

Triggers: Things that can bother you and change your emotional state.

Underbite: When your bottom teeth stick out farther than your top teeth.

Urethral opening: The small circular opening right below your clitoris that holds your urine.

Uterus: A hollow, pear-shaped organ in your body. Also known as the womb. This organ is where babies grow!

UV rays: Ultraviolet rays from the sun.

UVB rays: Type b ultraviolet rays from the sun.

Vagina opening: The muscular canal leading from your external to your internal genitalia.

Vaginal discharge: A sticky white or clear fluid that comes out of your vaginal opening.

Vaginal infection: A condition that causes your vagina to become inflamed and irritated.

Vulva: The outer skin of your genitalia.

Waxing: When you use wax or hot sugar to remove hair from your body.

Whiteheads: Tend to happen when your skin cannot breathe. Just like you, your skin needs oxygen too! Dirt can get trapped in the skin and without air, the bacteria can turn white, causing a small white bump. A medical term used for a primary sign of acne is called comedones (skin-colored bumps). Whiteheads are the result of closed comedones.

Withdrawn: A feeling of not being understood, resulting in isolation from family and friends.

Yeast infection: When too much yeast is produced in the vagina. This can be due to overactive hormones, not properly drying the vagina, or the foods that you eat. Signs of a yeast infection are inflammation (or burning sensation) inside of the vagina and during urination; thick, cottage-cheese discharge; and vaginal itchiness.

DAILY CHECK-IN &
SELF-LOVE AFFIRMATIONS

DAILY CHECK-IN & SELF-LOVE AFFIRMATIONS

DAILY CHECK-IN & SELF-LOVE AFFIRMATIONS

DAILY CHECK-IN & SELF-LOVE AFFIRMATIONS

DAILY CHECK-IN & SELF-LOVE AFFIRMATIONS

DAILY CHECK-IN &
SELF-LOVE AFFIRMATIONS

DAILY CHECK-IN &
SELF-LOVE AFFIRMATIONS

DAILY CHECK-IN &
SELF-LOVE AFFIRMATIONS

DAILY CHECK-IN &
SELF-LOVE AFFIRMATIONS

DAILY CHECK-IN &
SELF-LOVE AFFIRMATIONS

DAILY CHECK-IN & SELF-LOVE AFFIRMATIONS

DAILY CHECK-IN &
SELF-LOVE AFFIRMATIONS

DAILY CHECK-IN &
SELF-LOVE AFFIRMATIONS

DAILY CHECK-IN & SELF-LOVE AFFIRMATIONS

DAILY CHECK-IN &
SELF-LOVE AFFIRMATIONS

DAILY CHECK-IN &
SELF-LOVE AFFIRMATIONS

"NOTE TO PARENTS" BY DR. CHAMBERS

I first connected with Shanicia when she invited me to be part of her annual Period Party, an event that she curated to normalize the conversation around periods for girls. As with most of her work, it began with her personal life, her journey of explaining periods and puberty to her own daughter, and it then transformed into a desire to help other mothers and daughters do the same. Her work resonated with me on many levels. As a pediatric gynecologist, I'd also recognized the need for earlier period education and was working to provide this via my online platform, *The Period Doctor*. Her invitation to speak at her event allowed me to discuss anatomy, physiology, period products, self-care, and self-esteem. It was during this event that I realized just how many people Shanicia impacts and just how dedicated she is to the dual mission of empowerment and liberation around menstruation.

Shanicia's dedication to reproductive education is also evident through her global parenting community, *The Black Moms Blog*, and her book, *Oh Sis, You're Pregnant!* In that book, she speaks specifically to the experience of being Black and pregnant, and how to navigate pregnancy and motherhood with wisdom, strength, support, and sisterhood. Somehow, she manages to provide the reader with sisterhood in book form.

If her first book is gift of sisterhood, this period journal is like the gift of a village, one that lovingly ushers you into puberty and periods with knowledge, understanding, and celebration. She covers topics like breast development and personal hygiene while also providing structured space for daily check-ins and affirmations of self-love. She keeps the reader engaged with short, easy-to-follow formatting, punctuated by fun and interactive quizzes. The information is presented in a way that is relatable, honest, accurate, and empowering.

For too long, periods have been regarded as a source of shame, embarrassment, and even inferiority. This has been perpetuated by generations of mothers and grandmothers who have had to parent with inadequate tools and inaccurate information. Shanicia is rewriting the narrative around periods and placing the power in the reader's hands with shame-free guidance, embarrassment-proof information, and empowering conversation that can be accessed right in the comfort of their home.

The true beauty of this work lies in the assurance that the impact of this journal will reach well beyond the girl reading it. Because of the knowledge that she will gain, her friends, family, romantic partners, and potential future children will all have a chance at a better understanding of puberty and periods. Change requires one person. Sustained change requires a village. Thank you, Shanicia, for the gift of a village.

ABOUT THE AUTHOR

Shanicia Boswell is an advocate for Black parenting, diversity, and helping women learn to put themselves first, in the midst of running her global parenting community of over half a million women, Black Moms Blog, and retreat company, The Self Care Retreats. Her bestselling book, *Oh Sis, You're Pregnant!* was released as the #1 new release in Pregnancy and Childbirth and in Minority Demographic Studies on Amazon. Her passion and dedication has made her a sought out expert on parenting and self love. Shanicia has interviewed notable figures such as Michelle Obama and Meena Harris. Boswell's perspective on motherhood and womanhood have been featured on several publications, including OWN Network, The New York Times, and Washington Post. Shanicia has served as a panelist and speaker for notable conferences such as the Wellness Your Way Festival by Kroger and Proctor & Gamble, 21Ninety, and The Momference. She lives in Atlanta, GA.